# table of Contents

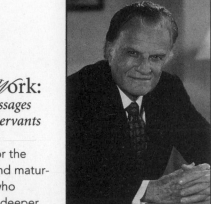

### Billy Graham

wrote the lessons in the Study Theme *The Secret of Happiness,* which is based on the Beatitudes in Jesus' Sermon on the Mount as recorded in Matthew's Gospel.

Dr. Graham is a world-renowned evangelist, preacher, and author. He is the founder of the *Billy Graham Evangelistic Association* in Minneapolis, Minnesota. He and his wife Ruth live in Montreat, North Carolina.

**BETTY HASSLER,** Ph.D., Biblical and Instructional Specialist in Leadership and Adult Publishing at LifeWay, wrote the personal learning activities and teaching plans this quarter.

## ABOUT THIS STUDY

**Are you searching for true contentment and joy? Do you find it an elusive goal?**

**List some things, events, or people that make you happy?**

**How long does this happiness usually last?** (circle)

a few hours          a few days          a few weeks

**Why do you think your happiness doesn't last longer?**

The seven lessons in this study will help you discover the source of happiness and all that flows from that source. Not only will you know the secret of happiness, but you will be equipped to apply biblical principles to your everyday experiences.

You may ask, How could poverty of spirit, meekness, or persecution possibly produce happiness? Good question! Now read the Study Theme Introduction and start with the first lesson for more clues.

---

### masterWork:
*Essential Messages from God's Servants*

• Designed for the developing and maturing believer who desires to go deeper into the spiritual truths of God's Word.

• Ideal for many types of Bible study groups.

• A continuing series from leading Christian authors and their key messages.

• Based on LifeWay's well-known, interactive model for daily Bible study.

• Teaching plans follow each lesson to help facilitators guide learners through lessons.

• Published quarterly.

ESSENTIAL MESSAGES FROM GOD'S SERVANTS

# masterWork

*Lessons from*

## THE SECRET OF HAPPINESS

### by Billy Graham

## LIVING ABOVE THE LEVEL OF MEDIOCRITY

### by Charles Swindoll

**FALL** *2003*

**LifeWay**
CHURCH RESOURCES
*Biblical Solutions for Life*

**GENE MIMS,** *President*

*LifeWay Church Resources*

**Ross H. McLaren**

*Editor-in-Chief*

**René A. Holt**

*Copy Editor*

**Brent Bruce**

*Graphic Design Specialist*

**Melissa Finn**

*Lead Technical Specialist*

**John McClendon**

**Mic Morrow**

*Adult Ministry Specialists*

**Send questions/comments to**

**Editor,** *MasterWork*

**One LifeWay Plaza**

**Nashville, TN 37234-0175**

**Or make comments on the web at**

*www.lifeway.com*

**Management Personnel**

**Louis B. Hanks,** *Director*

*Publishing*

**Gary Hauk,** *Director*

*Leadership and Adult Publishing*

**Bill Craig,** *Managing Director*

*Leadership and Adult Publishing*

**Alan Raughton,** *Director*

*Church Strategies*

Unless otherwise indicated, all Scripture quotations in the lessons from *The Secret of Happiness* are from the *King James Version*.

This translation is available in a Holman Bible and can be ordered through LifeWay Christian Stores. Unless otherwise indicated, all Scripture quotations in the lessons from *Living Above the Level of Mediocrity* are from the *New American Standard Bible*. © The Lockman Foundation, 1960, 1962, 1963, 1968, 1971, 1972, 1973, 1975, 1977. Quotations in the "How to Become a Christian" article or those marked HCSB are from the *Holman Christian Standard Bible,* © Copyright 2000 by Broadman & Holman Publishers. Used by permission. This translation is available in a Holman Bible and can be ordered through LifeWay Christian Stores. Quotations marked AMP are from *The Amplified Bible, Old Testament.* Copyright © 1962, 1964 by Zondervan Publishing House. Used by permission. Quotations from *The Amplified New Testament* © The Lockman Foundation 1954, 1958, 1987. Used by permission. Verses marked *Living Bible* are taken from *The Living Bible.* Copyright © Tyndale House Publishers, Wheaton, Illinois, 1971. Used by permission. Passages marked NASB are from the *New American Standard Bible.* © The Lockman Foundation, 1960, 1962, 1963, 1968, 1971, 1972, 1973, 1975, 1977, 1995. Used by permission. This translation is available in a Holman Bible and can be ordered through Lifeway Christian Stores. Quotations marked NIV are from the Holy Bible, *New International Version,* copyright © 1973, 1978, 1984 by International Bible Society. This translation is available in a Holman Bible and can be ordered through Lifeway Christian Stores. Quotations marked RSV are from the *Revised Standard Version of the Bible,* copyright 1946, 1952, © 1971, 1973 by the Division of Christian Education of the National Council of Churches of Christ in the U.S.A., and used by permission.

*MasterWork: Essential Messages from God's Servants* (ISSN 1542-703X) is published quarterly by LifeWay Christian Resources of the Southern Baptist Convention, One LifeWay Plaza, Nashville, Tennessee 37234; James T. Draper, Jr., President, and Ted Warren, Executive Vice-President. © Copyright 2003 LifeWay Christian Resources of the Southern Baptist Convention. All rights reserved. Single subscription to individual address, $26.35 per year. If you need help with an order, WRITE LifeWay Church Resources Customer Service, One LifeWay Plaza, Nashville, Tennessee 37234-0113; For subscriptions, FAX (615) 251-5818 or EMAIL *subscribe@lifeway.com.* For bulk shipments mailed quarterly to one address, FAX (615) 251-5933 or EMAIL *CustomerService@lifeway.com.* Order ONLINE at *www.lifeway.com.* Mail address changes to: *MasterWork,* One LifeWay Plaza, Nashville, TN 37234-0113.

Printed in the United States of America.

Cover image by Corbis

# The Secret of
# Happiness

The more I read the Beatitudes in Matthew's Gospel, meditated on them, and studied them, the more I realized that Jesus Christ was giving a formula for personal happiness that applied to anyone, no matter what his or her race, geographical situation, age, or circumstance.

The Beatitudes are revolutionary! Startling! Deeply profound, and yet amazingly simple! If applied on a universal scale, they could transform the world in which we live.

If you, dear reader, apply these simple formulae in your own personal life, you can never be the same! It is my prayer that as you study this material, and as you read and meditate on the Beatitudes themselves, you will realize that these ancient truths are as modern as tomorrow. They can change your life and point the way to true and lasting happiness—because they will point you to Jesus Christ and His timeless principles for living.

These seven lessons will help you understand the secret of happiness as revealed by Jesus.

"The Search for Happiness" (Sept. 7) is an introductory lesson that deals with people's search for happiness and what true happiness is. It invites us on a journey with Jesus to find true happiness.

"Poverty" (Sept. 14) explains the connection between spiritual poverty and the riches Christ has to offer us.

"Mourning" (Sept. 21) focuses on the mourning of inadequacy, repentance, love, soul travail, suffering, and bereavement.

"Meekness and Righteousness" (Sept. 28) highlights the meaning and traits of meekness and righteousness. It also examines four stumbling blocks to righteousness.

"Mercy and Purity" (Oct. 5) explores mercy in action and moral purity in mind and actions.

"Peacemaking" (Oct. 12) introduces us to being peacemakers in our homes, communities, churches, and workplaces.

"Persecution" (Oct. 19) teaches Christians to expect suffering and to endure it with patience. Suffering persecution is a believer's privilege and a source of blessing.

# The Search for Happiness

day One

> *Blessed (happy, to be envied, and spiritually prosperous—with life-joy and satisfaction in God's favor and salvation, regardless of their outward conditions) are the poor in spirit. . . .*　　　Matthew 5:3, AMP

## Looking for Happiness

*Happiness* is . . .

**How would you define happiness? Write your definition in the margin. Be prepared to share your answer with your group.**

A French philosopher said, "The whole world is on a mad quest for security and happiness." A former president of Harvard University observed, "The world is searching for a creed to believe and a song to sing."

A Texas millionaire confided, "I thought money could buy happiness—I have been miserably disillusioned." A famous film star broke down: "I have money, beauty, glamour, and popularity. I should be the happiest woman in the world, but I am miserable. Why?" One of Britain's top social leaders said, "I have lost all desire to live, yet I have everything to live for. What is the matter?"

The poet Amy Wilson Carmichael wrote:

> *The lonely, dreary road he trod.*
> *"Enter into my joy," said God.*
> *The sad ascetic shook his head,*
> *"I've lost all taste for joy," he said.*

A man went to see a psychiatrist. "Doctor, I am lonely, despondent, and miserable. Can you help me?" The psychiatrist suggested that he go see a famous clown at the circus who was said to make even the most despondent laugh with merriment. His patient said, "I am that clown."

A college senior said, "I am twenty-three. I have lived through enough experiences to be old, and I am already fed up with life."

A famous Grecian dancer of a generation ago once said, "I have never been alone but what my hands trembled, my eyes filled with tears, and my heart ached for peace and happiness I have never found."

One of the world's great statesmen said to me, "I am an old man. Life has lost all meaning. I am ready to take a fateful leap into the unknown. Young man, can you give me a ray of hope?"

**Do any of the following seem to be the sources of misery for these people?** (circle)

financial setback    drugs/alcohol    illness    peer pressure

marital trouble    lack of a job    reputation

**If not, what seems to be missing in their lives?** _____

_____

**Have you ever lost rays of hope in your life?** ❑ no ❑ yes

The Christian has a different perspective on the meaning of happiness. C. S. Lewis said, "Joy is the serious business of heaven." He added, "All His [God's] biddings are joys." Mother Teresa of Calcutta said, "True holiness consists of doing the will of God with a smile."

Jesus declared, "I am come that they might have life, and that they might have it more abundantly" (John 10:10). Or again He stated, "These things have I spoken unto you, that my joy might remain in you, and that your joy might be full" (John 15:11).

**If your joy is not as full as it once was, what will it take to fill it to the top? Ask God to show you what might be lacking and then record your answer.**

_____

_____

"I denied myself nothing my eyes desired; I refused my heart no pleasure. My heart took delight in all my work, and this was the reward for all my labor. Yet when I surveyed all that my hands had done and what I had toiled to achieve, everything was meaningless, a chasing after the wind; nothing was gained under the sun" (Ecclesiastes 2:10-11, NIV).

7

# day Two

# Searching for Happiness
# in the Wrong Places

Over 2,500 years ago the prophet Isaiah looked out on a people who longed for happiness and security but were looking for it in the wrong places. They were running to the marketplace and to places of amusement, spending their money madly for things that brought them no permanent satisfaction.

Isaiah stood before them one day and gave them the Word of God: "Ho, every one that thirsteth, come ye to the waters, and he that hath no money; come ye, buy, and eat; yea, come, buy wine and milk without money and without price. Wherefore do ye spend money for that which is not bread? and your labor for that which satisfieth not? hearken diligently unto me, and eat ye that which is good, and let your soul delight itself in fatness" (Isaiah 55:1-2).

In this particular sermon, Isaiah didn't speak negatively and berate the people for their sins. He didn't grab the bottle from the drunkard's hand, he didn't lecture them about the evils of gluttony, he didn't shame them for their immoral practices. He overlooked that for the moment. He simply asked them: "Are you getting what you want out of life?" Why do you spend your money for that which is not bread and your labor for that which does not satisfy?"

If Isaiah were living today, he would probably stand at Forty-second and Broadway in New York, in the Loop in Chicago, or on Market Street in San Francisco, and simply ask the milling, restless throngs: "Are you getting what you want? Are you finding satisfaction?"

He would ask the actress, surfeited with fame and fortune but peering out on life hungrily: "Are you getting what you want?" He would say to the eminently successful financier who commands his fleets and controls his industries: "Are you getting what you want?"

He would say to the laborers and workmen of America who are enjoying the highest standard of living in history: "Are you getting what you want?" He would ask the youth of America: "Are you getting what you want?"

> "Why spend money on what is not bread, and your labor on what does not satisfy?" (Isaiah 55:2, NIV)

He would say to the consumers of America who have the best homes, the most comfortable furniture, the finest food, the cleverest gadgets, and the smoothest, most powerful automobiles: "Are you getting what you want?"

**Answer Dr. Graham's question for yourself. Are you getting what you want?**

❑ yes ❑ sometimes ❑ usually ❑ no

**Why?** _____

# God Has the Answer

Isaiah did not leave his hearers with an unanswered question. He went on to tell them that there is a satisfying way of life, if they would seek it. He exhorted them to abandon their vain searching for pots of gold at the end of mythical rainbows, and to start searching for happiness where it is really found, in a right relationship with God.

Our materialistic world rushes on with its eternal quest for the fountain of happiness! The more knowledge we acquire, the less wisdom we seem to have. The more economic security we gain, the more bored and insecure we become. The more worldly pleasure we enjoy, the less satisfied and contented we are with life. We are like a restless sea, finding a little peace here and a little pleasure there, but nothing permanent and satisfying. So the search continues! Men will kill, lie, cheat, steal, and go to war to satisfy their quest for power, pleasure, and wealth, thinking thereby to gain for themselves and their particular group peace, security, contentment, and happiness, and yet in vain.

Yet inside us a little voice keeps saying, "We were not meant to be this way—we were meant for better things." We have a mysterious feeling that there is a fountain somewhere that contains the happiness that makes life worthwhile. We keep saying to ourselves that somewhere, sometime we will stumble onto the secret. Sometimes we feel that we have obtained it—only to find it illusive, leaving us disillusioned, bewildered, unhappy, and still searching.

**King Solomon certainly had every earthly reason to be happy. Complete the activity in the margin. Was the king getting what he wanted?**

**Read Ecclesiastes 1:14-18. Underline how you feel about King Solomon's conclusions.**

1. All of life is meaningless.

2. Many things about life seem meaningless.

3. Despite a few meaningless tasks, I find joy in life.

4. Joy can be found in all of life if you let God show it to you.

# Two Kinds of Happiness

There are, we need to realize, two kinds of happiness. One kind of happiness comes to us when our circumstances are pleasant and we are relatively free from troubles. The problem, however, is that this kind of happiness is fleeting and superficial. When circumstances change— as they inevitably do—then this kind of happiness evaporates like the early morning fog in the heat of the sun. In addition, even when our outward circumstances are seemingly ideal, we still may be troubled inside by a nagging hunger or longing for something we cannot identify. We say we are "happy"—but down inside we know it is only temporary and shallow at best. Yes, from time to time we may think we have found a degree of happiness, but sooner or later it will vanish. Our search for happiness remains unfulfilled.

**Circle the momentary kinds of happiness you have experienced.**

won a big game    got a good job    bought your first car

got a tax refund    got married    birthed a child

"Whoso trusteth in the LORD, happy is he" (Proverbs 16:20).

But there is another kind of happiness—the kind for which we all long. This second kind of happiness is a lasting, inner joy and peace that survives in any circumstances. It is a happiness that endures no matter what comes our way—and even may grow stronger in adversity. This is the kind of happiness to which Jesus summons us in the Beatitudes. It is happiness that can only come from God. He alone has the answer to our search for lasting happiness.

The happiness that brings enduring worth to life is not the superficial happiness that is dependent on circumstances. It is the happiness and contentment that fills the soul even in the midst of the most distressing of circumstances and the most adverse environment. It is the kind of happiness that survives when things go wrong and smiles through the tears. The happiness for which our souls ache is one undisturbed by success or failure, one that dwells deep within us and gives inward relaxation, peace, and contentment, no matter what the surface problems may be. That kind of happiness stands in need of no outward stimulus.

**Read each passage closely. Underline the passage only if it would not be possible to experience peace and joy in that circumstance.**

1. financial setback (Acts 4:32-35)
2. being martyred for your faith (Acts 7:59-60)
3. breaking an honored tradition (Acts 10:28)
4. peer disapproval (Acts 13:49-52)
5. going to jail (Acts 16:25)
6. illness (2 Corinthians 12:7-10)

In each one of the Beatitudes—which someone has called the "beautiful attitudes"—Jesus used the word *blessed.* This word *blessed* is actually a very difficult word to translate into modern English, because in the original Greek language of the New Testament it has a far richer meaning than the everyday content of our English word. The *Amplified Version* of the New Testament defines it as "happy, to be envied, and spiritually prosperous . . . with life-joy and satisfaction. . . ." But perhaps the word *happy* comes as close as any single English word to conveying the idea of "blessed" to us today, and that is the word we will use for the most part through this study. But let us never forget that the "blessedness" of which Jesus speaks is far, far deeper than any superficial happiness which comes and goes according to circumstances. That is why the word *blessed* guards well against its reduction and perversion.

Near to my home is a spring that never varies its flow at any season of the year. Floods may rage nearby, but it will not increase its flow. A long summer's drought may come, but it will not decrease. It is perennially and always the same. Such is the type of happiness for which we yearn.

**Do you have a spring, a place where you find stability in this unstable world? If so, thank God for this source of comfort.**

# Who Was This Jesus?

The Beatitudes are not the whole of Jesus' teaching, nor is even the Sermon on the Mount. (You can read the Sermon on the Mount in chapters 5–7 of the Gospel of Matthew.) There is much else that Jesus taught during the three short years of His public ministry. But Jesus was more than a great teacher. Who was this man Jesus, who never traveled outside His native Palestine and yet changed the entire course of human history?

Some have said that Jesus' main role was as a social reformer, coming to change society and liberate people who were bound by injustice and oppression. Others have said He came merely as an example, showing us by His acts of love how we should live. Still others have dismissed Him as a misguided religious reformer with no relevance to a modern, scientific age.

> "When Jesus came to the region of Caesarea Philippi, he asked his disciples, 'Who do people say the Son of Man is'? They replied, 'Some say John the Baptist; others say Elijah; and still others, Jeremiah or one of the prophets.' 'But what about you?' he asked. 'Who do you say I am?' "
> (Matthew 16:13-15, NIV)

But none of these are adequate to explain Jesus Christ as we see Him clearly pictured in the New Testament. The Bible, in fact, makes a startling assertion: Jesus was not only a man but God Himself, come down from the glory of heaven to walk on this earth and show us what God is like. Christ "is the image of the invisible God" (Colossians 1:15). More than that, He is the divinely appointed Savior who died for sinners, bearing their transgressions upon the cross.

He died to save all who had disobeyed God and who were slandering Him in their unregenerate natures. And He demonstrated beyond all doubt that He was the Divine Savior and Lord by being raised from the dead. The gospel is the good news of God "concerning his Son Jesus Christ our Lord, which was made of the seed of David according to the flesh; and declared to be the Son of God with power, according to the spirit of holiness, by the resurrection from the dead" (Romans 1:3-4).

The best modern scholarship is discovering once again that even the Sermon on the Mount, and the Beatitudes as well, cannot be isolated from the fact of Jesus' saviorhood. The Old Testament had taught that the Christ was to be meek. He was to turn mourning into joy; righteousness was to be His meat and drink; even upon the cross it was His deepest hunger and thirst.

**Read Isaiah 61:1-3. List five verbs that describe the actions of the coming Messiah. Keep your Bible open to Isaiah.**

_____     _____     _____

_____     _____

The coming Messiah also was the One who would show God's mercy to those who were separated from God in need. He likewise would be pure and without sin. Most of all, He would not flee the persecution that would come His way, but would bring peace—peace with God, peace within the human heart, and peace on earth.

**Read Isaiah 26:3-4.**
**How is perfect peace assured when we trust in the Lord?**

The Lord is _____.

In reality, Jesus Christ is the perfect fulfillment, example, and demonstration of Beatitudes. He alone, in the history of the human race, experienced fully what He tells us about the happiness and blessedness of life. What He tells us, He tells us as the Savior who has redeemed us and who is teaching His followers. But more than that, He is the One who gives us the power to live according to His teachings. Christ's message when He was upon the earth was revolutionizing and understandable. His words were simple yet profound. His words shook people. His words provoked either happy acceptance or violent rejection. People were never the same after listening to Him. They were invariably better or worse—better if they accepted Him, worse if they rejected Him. They either followed Him in love or turned away in anger and indignation. There was a magic in His gospel which prompted men and women to decisive action. As He clearly said, "He that is not with me is against Me."

**Drawing on your Bible knowledge, list three people whose lives were better after listening to Jesus. Then list three persons whose lives were worse after rejecting His words.**

_____     _____

_____     _____

_____     _____

# The Impact of Christlike Living

The world may argue against Christianity as an institution, but there is no convincing argument against a person who through the Spirit of God has been made Christlike. Such a one is a living rebuke to the selfishness, rationalism, and materialism of the day. Too often we have debated with the world on the letter of the law when we should have been living oracles of God, seen and read of all people.

It is time that we retrace our steps to the source and realize afresh the transforming power of Jesus Christ.

"Whosoever drinketh of the water that I shall give him shall never thirst" (John 4:14).

**Read John 4:7-14. What is the "water" that Jesus offered? Is it available to us today?**

_____

_____

This sin-sick, disillusioned woman is the symbol of the whole race. Her longings were our longings! Her heart-cry was our heart-cry! Her disillusionment was our disillusionment! Her sin was our sin! But her Savior can be our Savior! Her forgiveness can be our forgiveness! Her joy can be our joy!

# An Invitation to a Journey

**As we begin our study of the Beatitudes, read Matthew 5:1-2. Describe what you see as you contemplate the scene. Use your imagination if necessary. What kind of day was it? Who was there? Why were they there? Where were they?**

_____

_____

It's a hot, sultry day with the sweltering wind spinning little dust whirls and carrying them swiftly down the winding road by the Sea of Galilee. There is an air of expectancy in the atmosphere we breathe. The wind skips happily across the surface of the ancient sea. We hear voices raised in an excited, feverish pitch as friend calls a greeting to friend. Along every trail leading to Galilee little groups of people begin to gather. The word has spread abroad that Jesus is returning to Galilee.

Suddenly He and His little brand of followers emerge over the brow of a hill on the road to Capernaum, and immediately in their wake follows a vast multitude of people from Galilee, Decapolis, Jerusalem, Judea, and from beyond the Jordan River.

Quickly the word spreads from mouth to mouth. "Jesus is coming!" Other multitudes from Tiberias, Bethsaida, and Capernaum soon appear and join the others. Together they follow thirteen robed men. As they reach the summit of the hill where the gentle winds from the plains sweep over them, affording relief from the sun, Jesus stops and motions for them to sit down and rest.

The air is tense. It is a moment to be captured and held for eternity. The crowd hushes as Jesus climbs atop a large rock and is seated. In the valley on the deserted road, a lone camel rider wends his way along the trail toward Tiberias. A quiet falls upon the multitude as their faces gaze expectantly at Jesus. Then He begins to speak.

What He said there on that Mount of Beatitudes in faraway Palestine was to go down in history as the most profound, sublime words ever spoken! There in reverent, measured, simple words He revealed the secret of happiness—not a superficial happiness of time and space, but a happiness that would last forever.

His first word was *happy*. Immediately His listeners must have pricked up their ears.

> Jesus cordially invites you to come on an exciting journey with Him. Please respond ASAP to this invitation.

**Are your ears "pricked up" to hear what Jesus will tell you during this study? Pray the prayer printed below, or write your own prayer in the margin.**

*Father, Guide me on this journey to true happiness. I know true happiness is found only in You. Forgive me for seeking it in other people, things, success, and popularity. Give me a heart for You. Amen.*

Don't feel tied to the lesson plan. Be open to questions and comments from your group. Also, don't be distressed if you don't make it through the entire lesson plan. However, watch out for "chasing rabbits" or spending an undue amount of time dealing with one person's needs or issues.

NOTES

## Before the Session

1. Set up the room with chairs in a semicircle facing a focal wall. Plan to sit as a member of the group.
2. Place extra Bibles, copies of *MasterWork*, pens or pencils, name tags, and an attendance sheet on a table near the entrance.
3. You will need a writing surface, such as a chalk or marker board, tear sheets, or newsprint.
4. Since participants will not have had the previous week to prepare for today's study, this session will focus more on content from the book and will allow time to complete learning activities in class.

## During the Session

1. As participants arrive, direct them to sign the attendance sheet, prepare a name tag, and pick up a copy of *MasterWork: Essential Messages from God's Servants.* Encourage them to look through the book as others arrive.
2. Welcome participants. Acknowledge that many of us are currently facing situations, circumstances, or events that tend to rob us of our joy, such as loss of a job, finances, divorce in our extended family, illness, or loss of someone close to us. Ask members to pray for each other and for themselves throughout this study.
3. Lead in prayer. Introduce yourself and ask members to do the same. Then ask them to share what they find appealing about this study and what needs they hope will be addressed. Take notes as they talk and keep the list in mind as you continue the study.
4. Ask, *Why do people generally like telling secrets? Have you had a secret revealed? Have you told someone else's secret?* Then ask, *Why do you think Billy Graham chose to title his book* The Secret of Happiness?
5. Ask group members to turn to the table of contents in their copy of *MasterWork*. Review the seven lesson titles for *The Secret of Happiness*. Select a volunteer to read the biography of Dr. Graham ("About the Author").
6. Call attention to the main distinctions of *MasterWork* printed in the margin of that page. As a group complete the section titled "About This Study."

7.  Ask another volunteer to read the three paragraphs of Dr. Graham's study theme introduction on page 5. Then review the learning outcomes of the seven lessons. Ask members to place a check by the lessons that seem related to their life needs.

8.  Ask members to turn to Day 1 and complete the first activity by writing their answers in the margin. Invite volunteers to share their definitions. On a writing surface list the words *fun, pleasure, amusement, contentment,* and *joy.* Lead the group to distinguish these words from each other.

9.  Ask a volunteer to read the content of Day 2, "Searching for Happiness in the Wrong Places," stopping at the question, "Are you getting what you want?" Discuss how most adults would answer this question today.

10. Ask another volunteer to read "God Has the Answer." Form groups of two to three and assign them to complete the activity from Ecclesiastes 1:14-18. Allow 5 minutes.

11. In Day 3 explain the difference between the two kinds of happiness. Assign the Bible passages in the second activity to individuals to read aloud. Complete the activity as a group.

12. Ask members to turn to Day 4. On a writing surface list ways Jesus has been inaccurately described as members call them out (great teacher, social reformer, a good example, misguided religious reformer). One by one ask the class to refute these ideas. Then ask, *What are some proofs that Jesus is the Messiah, the God-Man?*

13. Invite volunteers to read the two Isaiah passages on page 13. Read the paragraph that follows the second activity. Have members complete the third activity as a group.

14. Ask a volunteer to read Matthew 5:1-2. Summarize "An Invitation to a Journey." Ask the question that concludes Day 5.

15. Assign the lesson for September 14. Ask member to read and complete the learning activities before next class. Close with prayer.

## After the Session

1.  Order additional copies of *MasterWork* if needed (see p. 2).
2.  Pray for your group members by name.
3.  Prepare for the next session by daily reading the lesson content and completing the learning activities. Then follow the suggestions in "Before the Session" in the Leader Guide that follows the lesson. Use "During the Session" to continue your lesson plan preparation.

# Poverty

*Blessed are the poor in spirit: for theirs is the kingdom of heaven.* Matthew 5:3

## Poverty in the World

**In your part of the world, is poverty a major problem?**
❑ yes ❑ no

**How does it impact you?** ❑ not at all ❑ some ❑ a lot

Through the media, we have all been made aware of the abject, hopeless poverty in much of the world. We have seen the starving in Africa, the displaced persons of Southeast Asia.

I myself have traveled in more than sixty countries of the world, many of them hopelessly buried in poverty. I have returned from cities like Calcutta with a heavy heart, wondering if anything can ever be done to alleviate their suffering.

Throughout the world I have found many Mother Teresas. Still, the poverty is virtually untouched. We have sent our own contributions through reliable relief organizations.

Yet under the filth, the starvation, the abject poverty I have sensed an even greater poverty—the poverty of the soul.

**If you had only two choices, which would you rather be?**
❑ physically, materially poor ❑ spiritually poor

On that day two thousand years ago, there were undoubtedly in that throng who heard Jesus speak, many who believed—as many today believe—that the key to happiness is to be found in wealth and possessions. As they gathered to listen to Jesus, perhaps they wondered if His words could actually make any difference to them in their search for happiness—as you may wonder. It was soon clear to them that Jesus' message was unique, for He was pointing another way to happiness—God's way. And it was a message that applied to every person.

When Jesus opened His mouth, the first word to fall from His lips was *happy*. Quickly on the heels of that first word followed five others: "Happy are the poor in spirit." If Jesus had omitted the last two words, they would have all rejoiced, for they were all poor—even if they would have been puzzled at how their grinding poverty could possibly make them happy. But Jesus said "the poor in spirit."

Wondering, they listened as He went on. Hidden in these seemingly cryptic words was the first foundational secret of happiness. At first it sounds like a contradiction. We usually think of people who are poor as being unhappy. But Jesus teaches that happiness can be found in spite of poverty.

**Why do you think wealth and possessions do not produce happiness?**

_____

_____

What kind of poverty did Jesus have in mind? Did He mean those who had very little of this world's goods? No. Certainly they were included. But Jesus was speaking to persons of every type—rich or poor, sick or well, educated or uneducated, young or old. God is concerned about every person on this planet, and Jesus' words were addressed to all persons, in every circumstance, and in every generation. They are addressed to you and me today.

**Perhaps you already know the full meaning of "poor in spirit." In Day 2 Dr. Graham will explain this phrase more fully. Read 2 Corinthians 8:9 in the margin. Write a paraphrase of this verse. Then thank God for His gift of grace through Christ that enables us to trade our poverty for His riches.**

"You know the grace of our Lord Jesus Christ, that though he was rich, yet for your sakes he became poor, so that you through his poverty might become rich" (2 Corinthians. 8:9, NIV).

# day Two

# Becoming Aware of Our Spiritual Poverty

What did Jesus mean by being "poor in spirit"? There are at least four dimensions to this crucial question.

FIRST: If we are to be poor in spirit, *we must be aware of our spiritual poverty.*

**To be poor in spirit:**

1. Be aware of our spiritual poverty.

The poor in spirit do not measure the worth of life in earthly possessions, which fade away, but in terms of eternal realities, which endure forever. Wise is the person who openly confesses his lack of spiritual wealth and in humility of heart cries, "God, be merciful unto me, a sinner."

> **This story illustrates "poor in spirit."**
> Jason was at the peak of his financial empire when the economy took a downturn and he was left with worthless stock. Jason began to cry out to God—something he had not done in years. Jason confessed his obsession with money and power.

My story of spiritual poverty

**Now in the margin write your personal story of a time spiritual poverty.**

In God's economy, emptying comes before filling, confession before forgiveness, and poverty before riches. Christ said there is a happiness in the acknowledgement of spiritual poverty that lets God come into our souls.

Now, the Bible teaches that our souls have a disease. It is worse than any dreaded cancer or heart disease. It is the plague that causes all the troubles and difficulties in the world. It causes all the troubles, confusions, and disillusionments in our own lives. The name of the disease is an ugly word. We don't like to use it. But it's a word that the psychiatrists are beginning to use once again. In our desire to be modern, we had almost forgotten it, but once again we are beginning to realize that it is the root of all human troubles. The word is *sin.*

We have sinned against our Creator. God is holy, righteous, and just. He cannot allow sin to enter His Presence. Consequently, sin has come between God and us.

**In the margin, illustrate the problem of sin by a drawing that shows how sin keeps us from God.**

Now, there must be a confession that we have broken God's laws and are willing to renounce our sins. We must acknowledge that without His fellowship life has no real meaning. This is not easy! All of us have pride, though it may be expressed in various ways. We do not like to confess that we are wrong or that we have failed. But God says: "All have sinned, and come short of the glory of God" (Romans 3:23). We must confess our sin as the first step to happiness, peace, and contentment!

Let us face this fact: We came into the world with nothing, and we will leave it with nothing.

Where do we get the notion that our idea of success and God's are the same? You have written a book; you are a clever manager and promoter; you are a talented artist; you are independently wealthy; you have achieved fame and fortune. Without the gifts of intelligence, imagination, personality, and physical energy—which are all endowed by God—where would you be?

Are we not born poor? Do we not die poor? And would we not be poor indeed without God's infinite mercy and love? We came out of nothing; and if we are anything, it is because God is everything. If He were to withhold His power for one brief instance from us, if He were to hold in check the breath of life for one moment, our physical existence would shrivel into nothingness and our souls would be whisked away into an endless eternity.

Those who are poor in spirit recognize their creatureliness and their sinfulness—but more, they are ready to confess and renounce their sins.

**Read I John 1:9-10. What are the subtle messages in the statements below that render them insincere apologies? Be prepared to discuss them with your group.**

1. "If I say 'I'm sorry,' that should be the end of it, right?"
2. "Saying 'I was wrong' is no guarantee it won't happen again."
3. "She has to forgive me because she's a Christian."

# Receiving Christ's Riches

**To be poor in spirit:**

1. Be aware of our spiritual poverty.

2. Receive the riches Christ provided.

We have seen that the first dimension of "poor in spirit" is a realization of our spiritual poverty. But can our poverty be overcome? Yes! And that leads us to the second dimension of what Jesus meant by being "poor in spirit."

SECOND: If we are to be poor in spirit, *we must receive the riches that Christ has provided by His death and resurrection.*

Would it not be wonderful if we could find an absolute cure for the troubles of human nature? Suppose we could give a shot in the arm to the whole human race that would fill us with love instead of hate, with contentment instead of greed. This would immediately solve all the problems that the world faces at this moment.

Suppose, also, a cure could be found for the past mistakes, failures, and sins of mankind. Suppose by some miracle all the past could be straightened out, all of life's tangles could be unraveled, and the broken strings of life could be repaired. Such a cure would cause a worldwide stampede!

**What personal problem from your past would you like to solve with a miracle cure?** _____

The most thrilling news in all the world is the fact that there is a cure! A medicine has been provided! People can be forgiven of all sin! The cobwebs that have collected in our lives can be removed!

The sin, confusion, and disillusionment of life can be replaced by righteousness, joy, contentment, and happiness. A peace can be imparted to the soul that is not dependent on outward circumstances. This cure was provided by Jesus Christ two thousand years ago on the cross of Calvary.

**Now place the problem you identified on the cross at Calvary. Nail it securely. Breathe the fresh air of joy, contentment, and peace.**

The cross has become a symbol in much of the Western world, misused by many rock stars and others who do not comprehend its significance.

The death of Christ on that first Good Friday was no mere accident. It was an act of a loving God to reconcile people to Himself. Sin had come between us and God. We could not be happy and contented apart from God. Therefore, in loving grace God sent His Son to bear our sins and to take the penalty and judgment that we deserved.

However, God requires something of us. We must confess our spiritual poverty, renounce our sins, and turn by faith to His Son, Jesus Christ. When we do that, we are born again. He gives us a new nature. He puts a little bit of heaven down in our souls. Our lives change. Contentment, peace, and happiness come into our souls for the first time.

**Perhaps you are still not free of anxiety about your identified problem. Nailing it to the cross requires faith to believe that Jesus paid for that sin once and for all. Read Hebrews 9:27-28 in the margin. Thank Jesus that you can leave your burden at the foot of the cross.**

"And just as it is appointed for people to die once—and after this, judgment—so also the Messiah, having been offered once to bear the sins of many, will appear a second time, not to bear sin, but to bring salvation to those who are waiting for Him" (Hebrews 9:27-28, HCSB).

In my travels I have watched for lastingly contented and happy people. I have found such people only where Christ has been personally and decisively received. There is only one permanent way to have peace of soul that wells up in joy, contentment, and happiness, and that is by repentance of sin and personal faith in Jesus Christ as Savior.

Has such a moment come to your life? Have you had the experience of receiving Christ? It is not simply an emotional experience. It is a simple surrender of the will to Christ. Do you really want happiness? Then you will have to pay the price of humbling yourself at the foot of the cross and receiving Christ as Savior.

**If you have not received Jesus as your personal Savior, please turn to the inside cover of *MasterWork*. There you will find information about how to claim the riches of a personal relationship with God through His Son Jesus Christ.**

**If you have made a decision to receive Jesus as your Savior, record that decision here. _____**

# Being Dependent on God

**To be poor in spirit:**

1. Be aware of our spiritual poverty.

2. Receive the riches Christ provided.

3. Depend on God.

We must know our spiritual poverty . . . we must turn to Christ in repentance and faith to receive His riches . . . but there is still more if we are to grasp the true meaning of being "poor in spirit."

THIRD: If we are to be poor in spirit, *we must be conscious of our dependence on God,* our spiritual bankruptcy.

Jesus said we must become like children before we can enter the kingdom of heaven. Children are dependents. That is to say, they depend upon their parents for protection and care. Because of their relationship and position they are not poor; but if it were not for their established relationship with their parents, they could be helpless and poor indeed.

When we come to Christ, a wonderful thing immediately happens to us. We become children of God! We become part of His family, as His sons and daughters! "As many as received him, to them gave he power to become the sons of God, even to them that believe on his name: Which were born, not of blood, nor of the will of the flesh, nor of the will of man, but of God" (John 1:12-13). In fact, the Bible uses the idea of "adoption" to illustrate this great fact. At one time we were alienated from God, with no rights or privileges. But in Christ we were adopted into His family (Ephesians 1:5-6). "For ye are all the children of God by faith in Christ Jesus" (Galatians 3:26).

**In the margin list some child-like characteristics that adults should cultivate to grow in dependence on God.**

As God's children, we are His dependents. The Bible says: "Like as a father pitieth his children, so the Lord pitieth them that fear him" (Psalm 103:13).

Dependent children spend little time worrying about meals, clothing, and shelter. They assume, and they have a right to, that all will be provided by their parents.

**Read Matthew 6:31,33 in the margin. In this passage from the Sermon on the Mount, what does Jesus indicate is the key to having our basic needs met? Underline it.**

"Take no thought, saying, What shall we eat? or, What shall we drink? or, Wherewithal shall we be clothed? . . . But seek ye first the kingdom of God . . . and all these things shall be added unto you" (Matthew 6:31,33).

Because God is responsible for our welfare, we are told to cast all our care upon Him, for He cares for us (1 Peter 5:7). Because we are dependent upon God, Jesus said: "Let not your heart be troubled" (John 14:1). God says, "I'll take the burden—don't give it a thought—leave it to Me."

Dependent children are not backward about asking for things. They would not be normal if they did not boldly make their needs known.

God has said to His dependent children: "Therefore come boldly unto the throne of grace, that we may obtain mercy, and find grace to help in time of need" (Hebrews 4:16). God is keenly aware that we are dependent upon Him for life's necessities. It was for that reason that Jesus said: "Ask, and it shall be given you; seek, and ye shall find; knock, and it shall be opened unto you" (Matthew 7:7).

**When you come to God's throne with a need, circle the words that would generally describe your attitude.**

bold      hesitant      hopeful      fearful

timid      confident      assured      cocky

What is troubling you today? Is your heart burdened because of some problem that threatens to overcome you? Are you filled with anxiety and worry about some problem, wondering what will happen? Listen: As a child of God through faith in Christ, you can turn these over to Him, knowing that He loves you and He is able to help you. At times He may take the problem away; other times He may give you strength to bear it. But you can rest in Him. "Have no anxiety about anything, but in everything by prayer and supplication with thanksgiving let your requests be made known to God. And the peace of God, which passes all understanding, will keep your hearts and your minds in Christ Jesus" (Philippians 4:6-7, RSV).

**If we keep our hearts and minds in Christ Jesus, what are we promised, even when the world doesn't understand? _____**

**Thank God for His wonderful promise!**

# day *Five*

# Denying Ourselves

**To be poor in spirit:**

1. Be aware of our spiritual poverty.

2. Receive the riches Christ provided.

3. Depend on God.

4. Deny ourselves.

As God's children we are not just meant to sit back and selfishly enjoy our privileges. Instead, God wants to use us to serve Him and help others. But before we can do that, something else must happen in our hearts if we are truly to know the full meaning of Jesus' words: "Happy are the poor in spirit."

FOURTH: If we are to be poor in spirit, *we must willingly deny ourselves that we might better serve Christ.*

**If you have read or heard the story of a Christian martyr, be prepared to share it with your group. In the margin, explain why martyrs seem so willing to give their lives for the cause of Christ.**

Reasons martyrs are willing to die for Christ:

The poor in spirit are those who are willing to sell out their stock in themselves and do as Jesus said: "Deny himself, and take up his cross, and follow me" (Matthew 16:24).

**How willing are you to obey Jesus' words?**
- ❏ 1. Show me the exit—quick!
- ❏ 2. I don't think I'll be put in that position in my lifetime.
- ❏ 3. I hope I'll have the courage to stand strong.
- ❏ 4. I am confident I'll do the right thing.

Our modern philosophy of self-reliance and self-sufficiency has caused many to believe that they can make the grade without God. "Religion," they argue, "may be all right for certain emotional people, but you can't beat a man who believes in himself."

The rich young ruler who came to Jesus was so filled with his piety, his riches, and his greed that he revolted when Jesus informed him that the price of eternal life was to "sell out" and come and follow Him. The man went away sorrowfully, the Bible says, because he could not detach himself from himself. He found it impossible to become "poor in spirit" because he had such a lofty estimate of his own importance.

All around us are arrogance, pride, and selfishness: These are the results of sin. From the heavens comes a voice speaking to a tormented, bankrupt world: "I counsel thee to buy of me gold tried in the fire, that thou mayest be rich; and white raiment, that thou mayest be clothed, and that the shame of thy nakedness do not appear; and anoint thine eyes with eyesalve, that thou mayest see. . . . Behold, I stand at the door, and knock; if any man hear my voice, and open the door, I will come in to him, and will sup with him, and he with me" (Revelation 3:18,20).

Heaven in this life and heaven in the life to come is not on a monetary standard. Nor can flesh and blood find the door to the kingdom of heaven with its contentment, peace, joy, and happiness. Only those who are poor in spirit and are rich toward God shall be accounted worthy to enter there, because they come not in their own merit but in the righteousness of the Redeemer.

### Which of these statements best explains "poor in spirit and rich toward God"? Underline it.

    a. I'm in a spiritual desert looking for an oasis of God's riches.

    b. I draw from God's strength out of my need and receive all of His abundance in return.

Someone has said, "A man's wealth consists not in the abundance of his possessions, but in the fewness of his wants." "The first link between my soul and Christ," said C. H. Spurgeon, "is not my goodness but my badness, not my merit but my misery, not my riches but my need."

Jesus said, "Happy are the poor in spirit: for theirs is the kingdom of heaven!"

### Can you list the four dimensions of "poor in spirit" that we have studied this week?

To be poor in spirit:

1. Be aware of our _____ poverty.

2. Receive the _____ Christ provided.

3. _____ on God.

4. _____ ourselves.

Adults enjoy a change of pace occasionally. If one of these learning activities is new to your group, try it more than once until it becomes familiar.

NOTES

## Before the Session

1. Decide which items from the personal learning activities in the lesson and which items from the teaching plan below you will use.
2. Place extra copies of *MasterWork* near the entrance.
3. Arrange for a writing surface in the room.
4. Find a "rags to riches" story in a book, on the Internet, in the public library, or in a newspaper. Be prepared to tell the story to the group.
5. Assign the Bible stories in step 2 below under "During the Session" to early arrivers to read and be prepared to tell in their own words.
6. On a writing surface on a focal wall print these Scriptures: Romans 5:8-11; 6:11; 8:17,37-39; Galatians 5:22-23; Ephesians 1:7-8; 3:18-19; Philippians 4:7,13,19; 1 Peter 2:24; 2 Peter 1:3; 1 John 5:4.

## During the Session

1. Welcome participants. Share prayer requests and lead in prayer.
2. Say, *Although our subject today is poverty, I'd like to tell a "rags to riches story I found in* (mention source)." Invite volunteers to share a similar story. Point out that the Bible has many "rags to riches" stories. Ask preselected members to tell these stories:
   a) Job (Job 42:12-17)
   b) A widow (1 Kings 17:12-16)
   c) Ruth and Naomi (Ruth 4:9-17)
3. Invite members to think about "rags to riches" in their spiritual lives. Form groups of 2-3 members each. Make this assignment: *What are some of the riches you have received as a child of the king?* Assign the Scriptures on the focal wall from Number 6 above to help groups identify some riches (or assign each group one of the biblical references from Number 6 above). Allow 5 minutes for group work.
4. Ask small groups to report their findings as you or a designated person lists the riches on a writing surface. Instruct the writer not to repeat a source of riches that has been listed already but to place a check by the same one as often as members name it.
5. Make the transition to the second beatitude by asking, *How many of you want to receive the riches we have listed from Jesus Christ?* (count hands) Then ask, *How many of you are willing to be spiritually poor?*

(count hands) *How many of you think there is a relationship between spiritual poverty and spiritual riches?* (count hands)

6. Say, *Spiritual poverty is often our state of mind when we become Christians. We recognize our need for God and our lack of strength in human relationships and victory over sin. However, once we become Christians, it's tempting to think we can take it from there, and we reduce God to an ally and partner rather than obey Him as our Lord.*

7. Acknowledge that many of us currently are facing situations, circumstances, or events that require God's supernatural power. When we come to God in our neediness, our spiritual poverty opens the windows of heaven and we receive His abundance in return.

8. Ask members to turn to Luke 18:9-14. Select three volunteers to read the passage—one to read the narration, another to read the words of the tax collector, and the third to read the words of the Pharisee. From this account lead the group to identify characteristics of spiritual poverty and lack of spiritual poverty.

9. Ask the group members to turn to Day 2 in their books. Invite volunteers to share their responses to the first two activities. Be prepared to share your answers as discussion starters. Then as a group review the insincere apologies from the last activity of Day 2.

10. In Day 4 members were asked to write child-like characteristics adults should cultivate to grow in dependence on God. As volunteers name these characteristics, list responses on a writing surface.

11. Discuss the relationship between denying ourselves and spiritual poverty. Ask, *In what ways are we called on to deny ourselves? How does self-denial strengthen us spiritually? When might it be simply "showmanship"? What does it mean to be rich toward God?*

12. Review and discuss the four dimensions of "poor in spirit" that were studied this week and their implications. Assign the lesson for September 21 for the next session. Close with prayer.

## After the Session

1. Do you have an unsaved or unchurched person in your class who may have prayed to receive Christ (final activity of Day 3)? If so, talk to him or her after class to clarify and follow up on the decision.

2. Begin reading next week's lesson and complete the learning activities. Follow the suggestions in "Before the Session."

3. Pray for each member of your class by name.

# Mourning

*Blessed are they that mourn: for they shall be comforted.*

*Matthew 5:4*

This second Beatitude, "Happy are they that mourn," at first seems paradoxical. Do crying and joy go together? How can we possibly be happy while we are in the throes of mourning? How can one extract the perfume of gladness from the gall of sorrow?

But rest assured that there is deep and hidden significance here, for remember, Jesus was speaking to all people of all beliefs and of all ages and was revealing to them the secret of happiness.

## The Meaning of Mourning

What did Jesus mean when He said: "Happy are they that mourn"?

**Mark T (true) or F (false). Someone who mourns:**
___  1.  is emotionally upset.
___  2.  takes a morbid view of life.
___  3.  shows great concern for others.
___  4.  lives a happier, fuller, richer life.
___  5.  cries a lot; wants to be left alone.

**Now check your answers in the paragraphs below.**

Certainly Jesus did not mean to imply that a special blessing is promised to "crybabies," "weeping Willies," or the emotionally upset. This verse was not intended to be a comfort for abnormal psychopathic cases, which have somehow become mentally warped and take a morbid view of life. No, it was addressed to normal, average people for the purpose of showing them how to live happier, fuller, richer lives.

Let us begin with the word *mourning* itself. It means "to feel deep sorrow, to show great concern, or to deplore some existing wrong." It implies that if we are to live life on the higher plane, then we are to be sensitive, sympathetic, tenderhearted, and alert to the needs of others and the world.

Define *mourning*.

The person who mourns is a person with a tender and sensitive heart. Let's look at some kinds of mourning that I believe were implied in this most significant saying of our Lord. We should ponder each one of them prayerfully.

Look for five types of mourning Dr. Graham discusses. Can you think of additional types of mourning?

Which type has affected you the most? Why?

# The Mourning of Inadequacy

First, there is *the mourning of inadequacy*. Jeremiah, the weeping prophet, mourned not in self-pity but for a wayward, lost world.

**In the margin, read what Jeremiah said.**

**What usually happens when we try to direct our own steps?**

_____

"I know, O LORD, that a man's life is not his own; it is not for man to direct his steps" (Jeremiah 10:23, NIV).

Before I can become strong, I must first realize that I am weak. Before I can become wise, I must first realize that I am foolish. Before I can receive power, I must first confess that I am powerless. I must lament my sins before I can rejoice in a Savior. Mourning, in God's sequence, always comes before exultation. Blessed are those who mourn their unworthiness, their helplessness, and their inadequacy.

Why is "the mourning of inadequacy" foundational to experiencing God's comfort?

Isaiah, the mighty prophet of God, knew by experience that one must bow the knee in mourning before one can lift the voice in jubilation. When his sin appeared ugly and venomous in the bright light of God's holiness, he said: "Woe is me! For I am undone; because I am a man of unclean lips . . . for mine eyes have seen the King, the Lord of hosts" (Isaiah 6:5).

We cannot be satisfied with our goodness after beholding the holiness of God. But our mourning over our unworthiness and sinfulness should be of short duration, for God has said: "I, even I, am he that blotteth out thy transgressions for mine own sake, and will not remember thy sins" (Isaiah 43:25).

Isaiah had to experience the mourning of inadequacy before he could realize the joy of forgiveness. If I have no sense of sorrow for sin, how can I know the need of repentance?

**In your own words, explain why spiritual growth depends on genuine sorrow for our sins. For assistance, read Psalm 34:18 in the margin.**

"The LORD is close to the broken hearted and saves those who are crushed in spirit" (Psalm 34:18, NIV).

_____

_____

In God's economy, a person must go down into the valley of grief before he or she can scale the heights of spiritual glory. One must become tired and weary of living without Christ before he or she can seek and find His fellowship. One must come to the end of "self" before one can really begin to live. The mourning of inadequacy is a weeping that catches the attention of God.

day Two

# The Mourning of Repentance

Another kind of mourning is *the mourning of repentance*. Following the consciousness that we are inadequate comes the awareness of the reason for our insufficiency—sin. As individuals we have no control over the fact of sin in the universe, but as creatures of choice we are responsible for its presence in our lives. Because "all have sinned, and come short of the glory of God" (Romans 3:23), all need to mourn the fact of sin in their lives.

The mourning of repentance is not the weeping of self-pity; it is not regret over material losses nor remorse that our sins have been found out. It is entirely possible to be deeply sorry because of the devastation that sin has wrought in our lives—and yet not repent. I have had people pour out their hearts to me with tears, because their sins have been discovered and they are in serous trouble. But true repentance is more than being sorry for our sins and regretting the way we have allowed sin to shatter our lives.

**What is the difference in these two phrases?**
1. I'm sorry if I . . . .          2. I'm sorry that I . . . .

_____

True repentance is a turning *from* sin—a conscious, deliberate decision to leave sin behind—and a conscious turning *to God* with a commitment to follow His will for our lives. It is a change of direction, an alteration of attitudes, and a yielding of the will. Humanly speaking, it is our small part in the plan of salvation—although even the strength to repent comes from God. But even so, the act of repentance does not win us any merit or make us worthy to be saved—it only conditions our hearts for the grace of God.

The Bible says: "Repent ye therefore, and be converted, that your sins may be blotted out, when the times of refreshing shall come from the presence of the Lord" (Acts 3:19). Our part is repenting. God will do the converting, the transforming, and the forgiving.

> " 'Even now,' declares the LORD, 'return to me with all your heart, with fasting and weeping and mourning' " (Joel 2:12, NIV).

**Is one sin more heinous to God than another? Explain your opinion.**

_____

_____

It will not be easy to bend our warped, stubborn wills; but once we do, it will be as though a misplaced vertebra has snapped back into place. Instead of the stress and tension of a life out of harmony with God will come the serenity of reconciliation. Our nerves will sense that our minds and hearts are relaxed, and they will send this happy news over their network to every fiber of our bodies. "Old things are passed away; behold, all things are become new" (2 Corinthians 5:17).

Just as pain precedes birth, mourning over sin comes before spiritual rebirth. I do not mean to imply that in everyone's experience there will be loud, violent weeping over the sin in one's life—sorrow for sin may come quietly, with little or no emotion. But there will be a sincere sorrow for the evils of one's life and a disposition to turn to God for help and salvation. The Bible says: "For godly sorrow worketh repentance" (2 Corinthians 7:10).

"Forgive us our debts, as we also have forgiven our debtors" (Matthew 6:12, NIV).

**The length or the brevity of our laundry list of sins is not the issue. The issue is maintaining our relationship with God. Sin breaks fellowship with God. Asking forgiveness restores that relationship. Seeking forgiveness from others is also critical to cultivating our relationship with God. Read Matthew 6:12 in the margin. Write the relationship between our being forgiven and our willingness to forgive.**

_____

_____

# The Mourning of Love

There is yet another aspect of this Beatitude, "Happy are they that mourn." There is, third, *the mourning of love.*

If I would know the measure of my love for God, I must simply observe my love for people around me. My compassion for others is an accurate gauge of my devotion to God.

This age in which we live could hardly be described as one in which people are honestly sensitive to the needs of others. We have developed a veneer of sophistication—but also cynicism and hardness. Our popular music talks about love, and yet divorce rates skyrocket, child abuse is rampant, and our world is shaken by wars, violence, and terrorism.

Much of the world is callous and indifferent toward mankind's poverty and distress. This is due largely to the fact that for many people there has never been a rebirth. The love of God has never been shed abroad in their hearts.

**Read these Scriptures. Beside each, write how the person expressed care for others after a personal experience with Jesus.**

1. Luke 8:38-39: _____

2. Luke 19:8: _____

3. John 4:39-42: _____

Jesus wept tears of compassion at the graveside of a friend. He mourned over Jerusalem because as a city it had lost its appreciation of the things of the spirit. His great heart was sensitive to the needs of others.

To emphasize the importance of people's love for each other, Jesus revised an old commandment to make it read: "Thou shalt love the Lord thy God with all thy heart . . . and thy neighbor as thyself" (Luke 10:27).

Many people speak of the social gospel as though it were separate and apart from the redemptive gospel. The truth is: There is only one gospel. Divine love, like a reflected sunbeam, shines down before it radiates out. Unless our hearts are conditioned by the Holy Spirit to receive and reflect the warmth of God's compassion, we cannot love our fellowmen as we ought.

**Do you remember how Jesus answered the question, "Who is my neighbor?" Read it again in Luke 10:30-37. Then, answer this question for yourself. Who is your neighbor?**

_____

_____

I am not as sensitive as I ought to be until I have learned the value of compassionately sharing others' sorrow, distress, and misfortune. Until then, I cannot know real happiness.

**On page 36 check your church's ministries that demonstrate compassionate caring for others. Put a double check by those in which you are a volunteer.**

❑ after school care    ❑ ESL program    ❑ clothing room

❑ travel assistance    ❑ prayer room    ❑ care-giver respite

❑ prison ministries    ❑ tutoring    ❑ tape ministry

❑ food pantry    ❑ disaster relief    ❑ home Bible studies

❑ rent, utility assistance    ❑ homebound Bible study

day *Four*

# The Mourning of Soul Travail

What is "soul travail," and how does it affect us? How has it affected you?

Another kind of mourning that brings comfort is, fourth, *the mourning of soul travail.*

This may seem cryptic, but it represents a very real and a profitable kind of mourning. The Bible says: "As soon as Zion travailed, she brought forth her children" (Isaiah 66:8).

We don't use this phrase "soul travail" very often, not as much as our spiritual forefathers a generation or so ago. Travail means "toil, painful effort, labor." "Travail of soul" therefore means spiritual toil—not necessarily outward labor that others will see, but that which takes place within the secret recesses of our souls. It refers to the continual flow of prayer that rises out of the Christian heart for a world that is spiritually unborn. And don't be under any illusions: This kind of soul travail is difficult and costly, because we are involved in spiritual warfare against Satan, the Enemy of Souls. "Pray without ceasing," the Bible says (1 Thessalonians 5:17).

"Pray continually" (1 Thessalonians 5:17, NIV).

"Pray constantly" (1 Thessalonians 5:17, HCSB).

**Read Matthew 4:1-3. Check your opinion below.**

❑ Spiritual warfare is just for super saints. I won't have to worry about it.

❑ That was just for Jesus. After all, He's the Son of God.

❑ If God turned Satan loose on Jesus, then I guess I'm in for it too.

❑ I'd better follow Paul's advice and pray earnestly as a lifestyle!

Before three thousand people were brought into the Church on the day of Pentecost, the disciples had spent fifty days in prayer, fasting, and spiritual travail.

John Knox, with an all-consuming soul-concern for his country, prayed: "Give me Scotland, or I die!" His earnest travail was rewarded with a spiritual rebirth in his land. This is what is termed "praying in the Spirit." It is the manifestation of a deep spiritual concern for others, and it is instilled by the Spirit of God.

The Bible says: "For we know not what we should pray for as we ought: but the Spirit itself maketh intercession for us with groanings which cannot be uttered" (Romans 8:26).

This kind of prayer can span oceans, cross burning deserts, leap over mountains, and penetrate jungles to carry the healing, helping power of the gospel to the objects of our prayer.

John Knox travailed in prayer, and the Church in Scotland expanded into new life. John Wesley travailed in prayer, and the Methodist movement was born. Martin Luther travailed, and the Reformation was under way.

God desires that we Christians be concerned and burdened for a lost world. If we pray this kind of prayer, an era of peace may come to the world and hordes of wickedness may be turned back. "As soon as Zion travailed, she brought forth her children" (Isaiah 66:8).

**Has God laid on your heart a specific prayer burden? If so, consider sharing it with your group at your next Bible study session. Join with others in united prayer, keeping in mind Matthew 18:20.**

"Where two or three are gathered together in My name, I am there among them" (Matthew 18:20, HCSB).

## day *Five*

# The Mourning of Suffering, Bereavement, and Despair

Another kind of mourning is *the mourning of bereavement.*

Nowhere has God promised anyone, even His children, immunity from sorrow, suffering, and pain. This world is a "vale of tears," and disappointment and heartache are as inevitable as clouds and shadows.

Suffering is often the crucible in which our faith is tested. Those who successfully come through the "furnace of affliction" are the ones who emerge "like gold tried in the fire." The Bible teaches unmistakably that we can triumph over bereavement. The psalmist said: "Weeping may endure for a night, but joy cometh in the morning" (Psalm 30:5).

Self-pity can bring no enduring comfort. The fact is, it will only add to our misery. And unremitting grief will give us little consolation in itself, for grief begets grief. Ceaseless grieving will only magnify our sorrow. We should not peddle our sorrows and bewail our bad fortune—that will only depress others. Sorrow, or mourning, when it is borne in a Christian way, contains a built-in comfort: "Blessed are they that mourn: for they shall be comforted" (Matthew 5:4).

There is comfort in mourning *because we know that Christ is with us.* He has said: "Lo, I am with you always, even unto the end of the world" (Matthew 28:20). Suffering is endurable if we do not have to bear it alone, and the more compassionate the Presence, the less acute the pain.

Yes, when a loved one dies, it is natural for us to feel a sense of loss and even a deep loneliness. That will not necessarily vanish overnight. But even when we feel the pain of bereavement most intensely, we can also know the gracious and loving presence of Christ most closely. Christ—who suffered alone on the cross, and endured death and hell alone for our salvation—knows what it is to suffer and be lonely. And because He knows, He is able to comfort us by His Presence. "Blessed be God, even the Father of our Lord Jesus Christ, the Father of mercies, and the God of all comfort; who comforteth us in all our tribulation, that we may be able to comfort them which are in any trouble, by the comfort wherewith we ourselves are comforted of God" (2 Corinthians 1:3-4).

> As you study today's lesson, underline the four reasons believers can experience comfort in the midst of mourning.

### Answer these questions about 2 Corinthians 1:3-4:

1. How does Paul describe God? _____

2. When does God comfort? _____

3. Why does He comfort? _____

4. What do we use to comfort others? _____

So, in our lives, there can be a blessedness in the midst of mourning. From suffering and bereavement God can bring into our lives new measures of His strength and love.

There is also comfort in mourning *because in the midst of mourning God gives a song*. God says in Job 30:9: "I am their song." In Job 35:10 Elihu asks, "Where is God my maker, who giveth songs in the night?" God's presence in our lives changes our mourning into song, and that song is a song of comfort.

In addition, there can be comfort in mourning *because God can use our sufferings to teach us and make us better people*. Often it takes suffering to make us realize the brevity of life, and the importance of living for Christ. Often God uses suffering to accomplish things in our lives that would otherwise never be achieved.

**Read James 1:2-4 below. Underline the product of tested faith.**

**What would be the result if our faith were not tested? We would be (check)**

- ❑ perfect
- ❑ imperfect
- ❑ incomplete
- ❑ complete
- ❑ lacking nothing
- ❑ lacking

The Bible puts it succinctly: "Count it all joy, my brethren, when you meet various trials, for you know that the testing of your faith produces steadfastness. And let steadfastness have its full effect, that you may be perfect and complete, lacking in nothing" (James 1:2-4, RSV).

Most of all, there is comfort in mourning *because we know that this life is not all, but we have the hope of heaven*. Paul said, "If in this life only we have hope in Christ, we are of all men most miserable" (1 Corinthians 15:19). But he knew that our hope was not just in this life, but in heaven. Our hope is in the resurrected Christ, who has opened the door to eternal life for all who put their trust in Him. "O death, where is thy sting! O grave, where is thy victory? . . . Thanks be to God, which giveth us the victory through our Lord Jesus Christ" (1 Corinthians 15:55,57).

How can the comfort of "the hope of heaven" avoid sounding like "pie in the sky by and by" to those who are mourning?

"Blessed (happy) are they that mourn." They are happy because they know that their aim, their distress, and their privation are the travail of a new creation, the birth pangs of a better world. They are happy because they are aware that the Master Artist—God—is employing both light and shadow to produce a masterpiece worthy of divine artistry. They are also made to glory in their infirmities, to smile through their tears, and to sing in the midst of their sorrow because they realize that in God's economy, "if we suffer, we shall also reign with him" (2 Timothy 2:12).

How have you experienced comfort in the midst of mourning? Be prepared to share an example with your Bible study group.

## Before the Session

1. Set up the room in the usual way.
2. Place extra supplies and the attendance sheet near the entrance.
3. Arrange for a writing surface in the room.
4. Draw a human outline on butcher paper and attach it to a focal wall. (Ask a friend, spouse, or class member to serve as a model. As he or she lies on the butcher paper, draw the outline of the body with a black magic marker. Masking tape will secure it to the wall.) Place several markers on the floor beneath the drawing.

## During the Session

1. Welcome participants. Share prayer requests and lead in prayer.
2. Ask someone to define the word *paradox* or use a dictionary definition (a truth that seems contradictory). Form two teams. Announce that each team has 30 seconds to state a paradox. The last team to identify a different paradox wins.
3. Point out that the second Beatitude, "Blessed are they that mourn," appears to be a paradox. How could mourning be a blessing? Ask, *Did you have any misconceptions about this Beatitude before you began your study of this week's lesson? If so, what were they?* Record responses on a writing surface.
4 Call attention to the human outline posted on a focal wall. Ask individuals to use the markers to list on the outline characteristics of those who mourn according to Dr. Graham. As starters, members may want to refer to the first activity of Day 1.
5. Invite a volunteer to summarize the characteristics that have been listed and to lead a prayer for members as they allow God to build these characteristics into their lives.
6. Form three groups and make the Scripture assignments below. Ask each group to identify how Jesus displayed the characteristics of one who mourns.
   #1: Luke 19:41-44    #2: Luke 22:39-44    #3: John 11:33-36

7. Ask, *Jesus was unable to demonstrate what characteristics of mourning?* (repentance, confession, restitution) Ask someone to read Hebrews 4:14-16. Ask, *Why is it important to us that Jesus did not sin?* Then ask, *How, then, can He comfort us when we mourn?*

8. Read the paragraph from Day 5 that begins, "Yes, when a loved one dies, it is natural for us to feel a sense of loss." Then read John 17:23 and Matthew 27:46. Ask, *What do you think Jesus may have been feeling when, for the first time, sin came between Him and His Father?*

9. Invite one or more to share what they wrote in response to the activity at the close of Day 1.

10. Ask for a summary statement from the group that will answer this question: *Why is love for God essential to love for any other person or group?* Write the statement on a writing surface easily seen by all.

11. Review the compassionate ministries of your church (end of Day 3). Optional: Assess the degree to which your church needs more involvement. Discuss ways to follow up on ideas from the group.

12. Read Matthew 18:20. Lead a discussion of responses to the last activity of Day 4. Encourage members to keep a record of these prayer burdens and pray about them through the remainder of this study.

13. From Day 5 discuss the bereavement ministry in your church. Does it reflect the spirit of 2 Corinthians 1:3-4? Direct members to answer the first activity of Day 5.

14. Read James 1:2-4. Discuss the activity on page 39. Then ask: *Why does God test our faith? What is the product of tested faith?*

## After the Session

1. Is there a follow-up action you need to take in regard to Step 11 above?

2. Begin reading next week's content and complete the learning activities. Follow the suggestions in "Before the Session."

3. Pray for each member of your class by name. Include the prayer burdens that were shared.

# Meekness and Righteousness

*Blessed are the meek: for they shall inherit the earth.*

Matthew 5:5

## The Meaning of Meekness

In this third Beatitude we have the words "Happy are the meek: for they shall inherit the earth." Has it ever occurred to you that there is happiness in meekness?

To most people today the word *meek* brings to mind a picture of someone who is a weak personality, someone who allows everyone to walk over him. Meekness, in fact, in the popular mind is not seen as a desirable personality trait.

The Greek word for "meek" was the word which was often used to describe an animal that had been tamed to obey the command of its master.

> "Those who follow the corrupt desire of the sinful nature and despise authority . . . are like brute beasts, creatures of instinct, born only to be caught and destroyed, and like beasts they too will perish" (2 Peter 2:10,12, NIV).

That is a vivid picture of what Jesus means by "meekness." When we are apart from Christ we are, in a sense, like a wild animal. We live according to our own desires and wishes, obeying our own instincts and ruling our own lives. But when we come to Christ our goal is different. Now we want to live for Him and do His will. This, after all, is God's will for us, for Christ "died for all, that they which live should not henceforth live unto themselves, but unto him which died for them, and rose again" (2 Corinthians 5:15). We are "meek," submissive to the will of our Master and ready to work for Him. And when our lives and hearts are marked by true meekness, we will know true happiness.

**On the next page, circle one or more areas of your life that Christ has tamed as a result of your becoming a Christian.**

tongue      thoughts      ears      lips

feet      tastes      touch

It is not our human nature to be meek. On the contrary, it is our nature to be proud and haughty. That is why the new birth is so essential to each of us. That is why Jesus frankly and pointedly said not only to Nicodemus but to every one of us: "Ye must be born again" (John 3:7).

Meekness begins there! You must have a change of nature. Do you want this happiness? Then you must be born again—this is the first step! If you are too proud, stubborn, and willful to take this first step, then you do not qualify to inherit the earth.

For help in learning how to be "born again," consult the article "How to Become a Christian" on the inside cover of *MasterWork.*

**The Bible has much to say about the vices of pride, stubbornness, and willfulness—all of which is unflattering. Capsule the main ideas of these verses. You will review these in your group session.**

1. Proverbs 8:13: _____

2. Jeremiah 9:23-24: _____

3. Matthew 23:11: _____

4. Romans 12:3: _____

5. 2 Peter 2:9-10: _____

**The Bible has much to say about being under Christ's control—a desirable goal. Match these Scriptures.**

____ 1. 1 Corinthians 6:19-20   a. Christ lives in me.

____ 2. Galatians 2:20   b. Christ is the Head.

____ 3. Ephesians 4:15   c. I am not my own.

____ 4. Colossians 3:1-2   d. My heart and mind should be set on things above.

# The Traits of Meekness

## GENTLENESS

The word *gentle* was rarely heard of before the Christian era and the word gentleman was not known. This high quality of character was a direct by-product of Christian faith.

The Bible says: "The wisdom that is from above is first pure, then peaceable, *gentle*, and easy to be intreated, full of mercy and good fruits, without partiality, and without hypocrisy" (James 3:17, emphasis added).

I have seen tough, rough, hardened men open their hearts by faith, receive Christ as Savior, and become gentle, patient, merciful gentlemen.

## YIELDEDNESS

*Yieldedness* is a trait of meekness. Those who are meek do not fight back at life. They learn the secret of surrender, of yielding to God. He then fights for us!

The Bible says: "For as ye have yielded your members servants to uncleanness and to iniquity . . . even so now yield your members servants to righteousness unto holiness" (Romans 6:19).

Instead of filling your mind with resentments, abusing your body by sinful diversion, and damaging your soul by willfulness, humbly give all over to God. Your conflicts will disappear and your inner tensions will vanish into thin air. Then your life will begin to count for something. It will begin to yield, to produce, to bear fruit. You will have the feeling of belonging to life. Boredom will melt away and you will become vibrant with hope and expectation. Because you are meekly yielded, you will begin to "inherit the earth" of good things which God holds in store for those who trust Him with their all.

"Neither yield ye your members as instruments of unrighteousness unto sin: but yield yourselves unto God, as those that are alive from the dead, and your members as instruments of righteousness unto God" (Romans 6:13).

**Do you tend to think of gentleness and yieldedness as primarily feminine virtues?** ❏ yes ❏ no

**What influences in society work against these character traits of meekness?** _____

_____

**How can we encourage gentleness and yieldedness as Christian virtues in our society?** _____

_____

In His wisdom God knows that an uncontrolled life is an unhappy life, so He puts reins upon our wayward souls that they may be directed into the "paths of righteousness." That is what God seeks to do with us: to tame us, to bring us under proper control so we can do His will.

"He leadeth me in the paths of righteousness for his name's sake" (Psalm 23:3).

**According to Dr. Graham, what is the likely fall-out if we do not allow God to bring us under proper control?**
- ❏ We will follow the right path.
- ❏ We can do God's will.
- ❏ None of the above.
- ❏ We will reign in our wayward souls.
- ❏ We will lead a happy life.

## FORBEARANCE

*Forbearance* is a word that has been almost dropped from our modern vocabulary. It means to abstain from condemning others, to refrain from judging the actions and motives of those about us.

The Bible says: "With all lowliness and meekness, with longsuffering, forbearing one another in love" (Ephesians 4:2).

Here is the Christian answer to neighborhood quarrels, to family fusses, and to community feuds: "Forbearing one another, and forgiving one another, if any man have a quarrel against any: even as Christ forgave you, so also do ye" (Colossians 3:13).

**Forbearance is not a common word in our vocabulary today. List synonyms, write a paraphrase, or use the word in a sentence to describe what the term forbearance means to you.**

_____

_____

### PATIENCE

"For ye have need of patience, that, after ye have done the will of God, ye might receive the promise" (Hebrews 10:36).

Ours is a high-strung, neurotic, impatient age. We hurry when there is no reason to hurry, just to be hurrying. This fast-paced age has produced more problems and less morality than previous generations, and it has given all of us a set of jangled nerves.

Impatience has produced a new crop of broken homes, a million or more new ulcers, and has set the stage for more world wars. In no area of our lives has it been more damaging than on the domestic scene.

But the Bible says: "Let patience have her perfect work, that ye may be perfect and entire, wanting nothing" (James 1:4).

Jesus Himself said: "Take my yoke upon you, and learn of me; for I am meek and lowly in heart: and ye shall find rest unto your souls" (Matthew 11:29).

**What is the relationship between your level of stress and your level of patience? (Place an X on the line.)**

no relationship      some relationship      high relationship

**Ask God to make you aware of opportunities for exercising patience today. See if it affects your level of stress.**

day Three

*Blessed are they which do hunger and thirst after righteousness: for they shall be filled.*

Matthew 5:6

# Happy though Hungry

It is not enough to be hungry and thirsty. The important question is, "What are you hungry for?"

Each of us was created in the image and likeness of God. We were made for God's fellowship, and our hearts can never be satisfied without His communion. Just as iron is attracted to a magnet, the soul in its state of hunger is drawn to God. David said, "As the deer pants for streams of water, so my soul pants for you, O God" (Psalm 42:1, NIV). Again David said, "O God, thou art my God; early will I seek thee: my soul thirsteth for thee, my flesh longeth for thee in a dry and thirsty land, where no water is" (Psalm 63:1). Isaiah said, "With my soul have I desired thee in the night; yea, with my spirit within me will I seek thee early: for when thy judgments are in the earth, the inhabitants of the world will learn righteousness" (Isaiah 26:9).

**Compare your thirst for human companionship to your thirst for God. Which is the stronger?**
❑ friend     ❑ God

**Which companionship do you nurture the most?**
❑ friend     ❑ God

# Righteousness

Any kind of religious experience that does not produce righteousness in our lives is a counterfeit and not worth seeking. So what is this righteousness that Jesus exhorts us to hunger for?

Many have tried to reform to gain favor with God. Some have mutilated their bodies and tortured themselves, thinking thereby to gain favor with God. Others have thought that if they would work hard and live moral lives, they could somehow justify themselves.

But the Bible teaches that all our righteousness—falling short of the divine standard as it does—is as filthy rags in the sight of God. There is absolutely no possibility of our manufacturing a righteousness, holiness, or goodness that will satisfy God. Even the best of us is impure to God.

"All of us have become like one who is unclean, and all our righteous acts are like filthy rags" (Isaiah 64:6, NIV).

**Read 2 Corinthians 10:12. When we compare ourselves to others, we may come off looking pretty good. Name two people you compare yourself to the most.**

_____     _____

**Read 1 Peter 2:21-24. Now how do you look? (Place an X on the line that best indicates where you stand.)**

|⊢⊢⊢⊢⊢⊢⊢⊢⊢⊢⊢⊣|

filthy rags                                    white robe

In spite of our sins and moral uncleanness, God loves us. He decided to provide a righteousness for us. On the ground of faith in the atoning death and resurrection of His Son, God has provided and ascribed righteousness for all who will receive it.

But when we come to Christ by faith and receive Him as our Savior, our "hunger and thirst after righteousness" are not ended.

It is not God's will for us to continue in sin—and, in fact, if we are completely indifferent to the presence of sin in our lives, the Bible indicates we do not really know Christ. Instead of continuing in sin, we are to "hunger and thirst after righteousness"—to pursue righteousness and purity with God's help, so that our lives become increasingly like Christ every day.

If you have a Bible dictionary, look up the meanings of "justification" and "sanctification."

The righteousness of the God-man is applied to us in justification and in sanctification, so that righteousness is progressively implanted in the believer's heart.

day *Four*

# Four Stumbling Blocks to Righteousness

**Four Stumbling Blocks to Righteousness:**

1. Sinful pleasure
2. Self-sufficiency
3. Secret Sin
4. Neglect of one's spiritual life

There are several things that can spoil our appetite for the righteousness of God.

FIRST: *Sinful* pleasure can ruin our appetite for the things of God.

Paul had a young co-laborer in the gospel named Demas. Because his appetite for the pleasures of the world was greater than his thirst for God, we hear very little of young Demas. Paul wrote his entire history in nine words: "Demas hath forsaken me, having loved this present world" (2 Timothy 4:10).

Many of us have no appetite for spiritual things because we are absorbed in the sinful pleasures of this world. We have been eating too many of the devil's delicacies. Our sins may be very obvious and open, or they may be very respectable or subtle. Perhaps we are preoccupied with material things which, while not wrong in themselves, have wrapped their tentacles around us and are squeezing out our spiritual hunger and thirst for righteousness. We may be preoccupied with our career or our education, or any of hundreds of other things that can dull our appetite for God and His righteousness.

SECOND: *Self-sufficiency* can impair our hunger after God. No one is so empty as he who thinks he is full. No one is so ill as he who has a fatal disease and yet thinks he is in perfect health. No one is so poor as he who thinks he is rich but is actually bankrupt.

The Bible says: "Thou sayest, I am rich, and increased with goods, and have need of nothing; and knowest not that thou art wretched, and miserable, and poor, and blind, and naked" (Revelation 3:17).

A person who is filled with himself has no room for God in his life. Self-sufficiency can ruin one's appetite for the things of Christ.

THIRD: *Secret sin* can take away our appetite for the righteousness of God.

That secret sin we commit has a price. We may think we've kept our sin a secret, but remorse for it will remain in our hearts. Those evil resentments we harbor in our minds against our neighbor! The failure to forgive those who have wronged us! When the heart is filled with wickedness, there is no room for God. The jealousies, the envies, the prejudices, and the malices will take away our appetite for the things of the Spirit.

FOURTH: *Neglect of our spiritual life* can take away our appetite for the righteousness of God.

All Christians believe in God, but nominal Christians have little time for God. They are too busy with everyday affairs to be concerned with Bible reading, prayer, and being thoughtful to their fellowmen. Many have lost the spirit of a zealous discipleship.

If you ask them if they are Christians, they would probably answer, "I think so" or "I hope so." They may go to church at Easter and Christmas and other special occasions, but otherwise they have little time for God. They have crowded God out of their lives.

The Bible warns us against neglect of our souls. It is possible to harden our hearts and shrivel our souls until we lose our appetite for the things of God. Just like someone who refuses to eat and eventually grows weaker and weaker until he dies, so a person who is "too busy" for God will starve himself and wither away spiritually.

**Is it possible to neglect your spiritual life and yet be involved in religious activities?**

❑ yes ❑ no ❑ I'm not sure

**What is the goal of our spiritual lives?**

❑ 1. to get to heaven

❑ 2. to earn our crowns in glory

❑ 3. to keep God off our backs

❑ 4. to get favors from God

❑ 5. to develop a love relationship with God

day *Five*

# The Secret of Surrender

Some time ago a policeman asked me what the secret of victorious living was. I told him that there is no magic formula that can be pronounced. If any word could describe it, I would say *surrender*.

Christ is calling Christians today to cleansing, to dedication, to consecration, and to full surrender. It will make the difference between success and failure in our spiritual lives. It will make the difference between being helped and helping others. It will make a difference in our habits, in our prayer life, in our Bible reading, in our giving, in our testimony, and in our church membership. This is the Christian's hour of decision!

But many ask, "How can I begin?" I would like to suggest that you take all of the sins that you are guilty of and make a list of them. Then confess them, and check them off, remembering that Jesus Christ forgives. The Bible says: "If we confess our sins, he is faithful and just to forgive us our sins, and to cleanse us from all unrighteousness" (1 John 1:9).

In addition, ask God to cleanse you from those sins you may not be aware of, and to make you more sensitive to the presence of hidden sins in your life—wrong motives, wrong attitudes, wrong habits, wrong relationships, wrong priorities. It may even be that you will have to make restitution if you have stolen anything, or you may have to seek out someone and ask his forgiveness for a wrong you have committed.

Then, after you have confessed every known sin in your life, yield every area of your life. Yield your girlfriend, your boyfriend, your family, your business, your career, your ambitions, your soul, the innermost thoughts and depth of your heart; yield them all to Christ. Hold nothing back. As the songwriter says, "Give them all to Jesus."

Take your eyes and your ears and your hands and your feet and your thoughts and your heart and give them completely and unreservedly to Christ. Then by faith believe that God has accepted your surrender.

**Are you willing to take these four steps recommended by Dr. Graham? If so, make some time available when you can be alone and do not have to be ruled by a clock. "Draw near to God, and He will draw near to you" (James 4:8, HCSB)**

If this is your hunger and desire, then God will do exactly what He has promised to do: He will fill you. "Happy are they that hunger and thirst after righteousness: for they shall be filled." Every promise God has ever made He has kept. He will fill you now if you are hungry enough to surrender.

We shall not be perfect in thought, word, and deed until we are glorified in the world to come, but the breath of that glory, and a god-likeness of character, is the Christian's proper heritage in this earthly walk. We are Christians, and the world should sense to its conviction that, wherever we walk in its midst, a heavenly virtue still goes out from whatever truly bears His Name.

**Do non-Christians sense that there is something different about you? If not, why not?**
  ❏ 1. I act pretty much the same way they act.
  ❏ 2. I don't like being singled out.
  ❏ 3. I'm afraid I'll be teased.
  ❏ 4. I've never seen this behavior modeled by another Christian.
  ❏ 5. Other? _____

**Steps to Surrender:**

1. List the sins you know you are guilty of and ask for forgiveness.

2. Ask God to reveal unknown sins to you and to cleanse you of them.

3. Make restitution whenever possible.

4. Yield every area of your life to God.

Are you reading from your Bible during each session? Are class members being encouraged to use their Bibles? Studying what the masters have drawn from God's Word is our focus.

NOTES

## Before the Session

1. On a focal wall display an attractive grouping of pictures of horses in several settings.

2. Find information on the Internet, in a library, or in other reference material on the process of taming a horse. Be prepared to briefly explain the process. Optional: Ask a class member to present this information.

3. Optional: Hand four early arrivers a slip of paper on which you have written one of the following traits of meekness: gentleness, yieldedness, forbearance, patience. Ask each to be prepared to discuss the character trait he or she received when called upon to do so.

## During the Session

1. Welcome participants. Share prayer requests and lead in prayer.

2. Ask volunteers to share insights they have gained from the study thus far. Be prepared to start the discussion. Record responses on a writing surface.

3. Ask a volunteer to read Matthew 5:5. Ask Dr. Graham's question from Day 1: "Has it ever occurred to you that there is happiness in meekness?" After several responses, allow volunteers to suggest other words that convey the idea of meekness.

4. Note the Greek meaning for the word *meek*. Point to the pictures of horses. Ask if someone knows the process for taming a wild horse. Fill in any missing information with the data you collected, or invite the member you pre-selected to give a report.

5. Form two groups and give assignments: Group #1: How are non-Christians like an untamed horse? Group #2: How are Christians to resemble a tamed horse? After 2-3 minutes, ask groups to report.

6. As time permits, invite examples (without being personal) of ways Christ can transform each body part listed in the first learning activity of Day 1.

7. Remind members that inheriting the earth requires being born again. The opposite is being too proud, stubborn, or willful to take this step.

8. Review answers to the Scripture activities at the end of Day 1.

9. Ask members to name the four characteristics of meekness from Day 2.

10. Optional: Ask the four individuals who received the traits of meekness to discuss their characteristics.

11. Inquire, *Is the word "gentle" often thought of as a feminine trait?* Have the group mention ways a man can be gentle, according to God's Word. Assign these verses to be read aloud: Isaiah 40:11; Matthew 11:29-30; and 2 Corinthians 10:1. Ask someone to characterize the image of Christ painted by these Scriptures.

12. Explain how we produce the fruit of yieldedness by leading a discussion of John 15:1-8. (Do not allow the discussion of this Scripture to lead the group astray into a discussion of eternal security.)

13. Compare and contrast the words *forbearance* and *patience*.

14. Call on a volunteer to read Matthew 5:6. Ask if someone has ever been truly hungry or thirsty, such as lost on a hiking trip. Have one or two share their experiences. Point out that hunger and thirst for God is to be for the purpose of pursuing righteousness. Ask, *What is the difference between "being righteous" and "pursuing righteousness"?*

15. Say, *1 John 1:8 assures us we will continue to sin as believers. Verse 9 gives us the process for asking and receiving forgiveness. However, a true believer will not commit the same sin as a continuous lifestyle choice.* Then ask a volunteer to read 1 John 3:6.

16. Review Dr. Graham's list of four stumbling blocks to righteousness. Ask learners who are willing to share with the group which of these affects them the most personally. Then as a group, discuss the learning activity in Day 4.

17. Ask a volunteer to read the plan for surrender Dr. Graham suggests in Day 5. Encourage members to complete the four steps in a private setting. Lead a prayer that all members would be more conscious of the fact that they bear the Lord's name wherever they go.

## After the Session

1. Is there a follow up action you need to take in regard to Step 17?

2. Read next week's content and complete the learning activities. Follow the suggestions in "Before the Session."

3. Pray for each member of your class by name. Include the prayer burdens that were shared during the group time.

# Mercy and Purity

*Blessed are the merciful: for they shall obtain mercy.*
Matthew 5:7

## Mercy Defined

In the Bible mercy refers to compassion, to pity for the undeserving and the guilty.

Perhaps no more beautiful illustration of mercy exists in the Bible (apart from God's mercy to us in Christ) than that of Joseph and his undeserving brothers. You recall how, through jealousy, the brothers sold Joseph into slavery, convincing his father that he had been devoured by wild beasts. In the following years Joseph, through his faithfulness to God and his master, rose in position in Egypt until he was second in power to Pharaoh himself. Famine drove the unsuspecting brothers down to Egypt to buy food. Where vengeance and just retribution were certainly justified, Joseph showed only mercy and lovingkindness (Genesis 50:20-21).

So, too, in our lives, we are to be merciful to those who have wronged us, hurt us, or even done incredibly cruel things to us. If we are submissive and loyal to God, we may see behind the unkindness and evil God's love working for our good and His glory.

> "You intended to harm me, but God intended it for good to accomplish what is now being done, the saving of many lives. So then, don't be afraid. I will provide for you and your children. And [Joseph] reassured them and spoke kindly to them"
> (Genesis 50:20-21, NIV).

**How does Dr. Graham define mercy?**

_____

**Illustrate an act of mercy from your life.**

_____

# Mercy Is Not Self-Centered

Jesus knew that one of the real tests of our yieldedness to God is our willingness to share with others. If we have no mercy toward others, that is one proof that we have never experienced God's mercy.

A body of water that has an inlet but no outlet becomes a stagnant pond. When we think of Christianity as *my* experience, *my* emotions, *my* ecstasy, *my* joy, *my* faith—with no desire to share mercifully with others—we can only boast of stagnation, not living, vital, flowing Christianity!

In this Beatitude, which we could well term the "outflowing" Beatitude, Jesus is emphasizing the fact that we are to be unchoked channels through which His love and mercy flow out to other people.

If we have a religion that does not work effectively in everyday life, one which fails to condition our attitudes toward our fellowmen and one which makes us spiritual introverts, we may be sure that we do not know the Christ who spoke these Beatitudes!

If we embrace a spiritual, aesthetic gospel only and disregard our obligation to our fellowmen, we annul it all. The gospel of the New Testament can come into full blossom only when the seed of the Spirit is buried in the rich soil of human mercy. The gospel is first an intaking, and then an outgiving. Jesus said in our outgiving we would find happiness.

> "If we have no mercy toward others, that is one proof that we have never experienced God's mercy."

**In the left column draw a stagnant pond of mercy kept only for oneself. In the right column illustrate Christ's love and mercy flowing out to other people.**

| Stagnant Pool | Outflowing Channel |
|---|---|
| | |

**Circle the name of the drawing that best reflects your life.**

# Mercy in Action

What are some ways we can show mercy in today's world?

FIRST: We can show mercy *by caring for the needs of others*. We should look around at our neighbors and see if any are hurting or in need.

Who is my neighbor? He who is closest to me—my husband or wife, child, parent, brother, sister, the person next door, the couple down the street. It is easier to be concerned with the deprived person halfway around the world, and ignore the needs of those closest to me—perhaps only a word of encouragement or appreciation. At the same time, we cannot ignore the needs of our fellowmen on a worldwide scale.

Did not Jesus feed the multitudes as well as preach the gospel to them? Did He not point out to us the folly of taking religion and failing to put it into action?

SECOND: We can show mercy *by doing away with our prejudices*.

I have been privileged across the years to visit many, many countries in every part of the world. However, I have never visited a country that did not have some problem with prejudice. At times it was prejudice against a racial or religious minority within its boundaries. At times it was prejudice against people from other nations. At times it was prejudice or resentment against those who were wealthier or those who were poorer than the average. But prejudice is a universal problem.

Prejudice is a mark of weakness, not of strength; it is a tool of the bigot, but never a device of the true Christian.

How can we get rid of this murderous prejudice? There is only one way we can get rid of prejudice: by the process of spiritual rebirth through faith in Christ. Only then do we discover God's love for all humanity, and only then will we begin to look at others through the eyes of God and see them as He sees them. Only then does God's love begin to take root in our hearts, pushing out the hate and indifference and selfishness that have resided there.

THIRD: We can show mercy *by sharing the gospel of Christ with others*.

The spiritual poverty of the world is not clear or even evident to us until we begin to look at it in the light of God's Word, the Bible.

**Ways we can show mercy in today's world:**

• by caring for the needs of others

• by doing away with our prejudices

• by sharing the gospel of Christ with others

"Prejudice is a mark of weakness, not of strength; it is a tool of the bigot, but never a device of the true Christian."

But when we begin to understand God's Word, we realize that the world is lost and under the judgment of God apart from Christ.

The fact that, after two thousand years of Christianity, more than half of the world's population still knows nothing about the saving, transforming grace of Christ should stir us to a renewed dedication to tell a dying world about the mercy of God. Jesus said: "Go ye into all the world, and preach the gospel to every creature" (Mark 16:15).

The mercy the world needs is the grace, love, and peace of our Lord Jesus Christ. It is His transforming and regenerating power that the world needs more than anything else.

William Shakespeare wrote:

> *The quality of mercy is not strained;*
> *It droppeth as the gentle rain from heaven*
> *Upon the place beneath: it is twice blest*
> *It blesseth him that gives and him that takes:*
> *'Tis mightiest in the mightiest; it becomes*
> *The throned monarch better than his crown.*

"The mercy the world needs is the grace, love, and peace of our Lord Jesus Christ."

No, the path to happiness is not found in selfish living and indifference to others. Instead, when we have experienced the mercy of God then we will show mercy to others. Then we will indeed be "twice blest" because we will both make others happy and experience true happiness ourselves. "Happy are the merciful: for they shall obtain mercy."

**From Dr. Graham's list of mercy in action, give an example of how you can show mercy this week by**

1. caring for someone's needs:

   _____

2. doing away with a prejudice:

   _____

3. sharing the gospel with someone:

   _____

*day Three*

*Blessed are the pure in heart: for they shall see God.*
*Matthew 5:8*

# The Meaning of Purity

The word that is translated "pure" in Matthew 5:8 was used in several ways in the original Greek language. For one thing, it was often used to mean something that was unadulterated or unmixed with anything foreign, such as pure gold that had not been mixed with any other metal, or milk that had not been watered down. Or again, it often simply meant "clean," like a dish that had been thoroughly washed or clothes that had been scrubbed.

Now apply those meanings to "pure in heart." If we are truly pure in our hearts, we will have a single-minded devotion to the will of God. Our motives will be unmixed, our thoughts will not be adulterated with those things that are not right. And our hearts will be clean, because we will not tolerate known sin in our hearts and allow it to pollute us.

There is, however, another dimension to this word *pure.* It also sometimes means something that was purged of wrong so it could be used for right. William Barclay points out that it could be used of an army that had been purged or cleared of soldiers who were cowardly or weak and unable to fight. It would then be a "pure" army, filled with dedicated and trained soldiers ready for battle. This would be like a person's body that is purified of sickness so it is strong and able to work. In the same way, when we are "pure in heart" we are ready to do those good things that God has for us to do.

In other words, purity of heart has both a negative and a positive side. On the one hand, our hearts are to be emptied of sin and its dominion over us. On the other hand, we are to be pure in our actions and filled with all that is pure. The Bible illustrates these negative and positive sides to purity: "Put to death therefore what is earthly in you: immorality, impurity, passion, evil desire, and covetousness. . . . Put them all away: anger, wrath, malice, slander, and foul talk. . . . Put on then, as God's chosen ones, holy and beloved, compassion,

> "Purity of heart has both a negative and a positive side. On the one hand, our hearts are to be emptied of sin and its dominion over us. On the other hand, we are to be pure in our actions and filled with all that is pure."

kindness, lowliness, meekness, and patience. . . . And above all these put on love" (Colossians 3:5,8,12,14; RSV, emphasis added).

**How does Dr. Graham define purity?** _____

_____

**Describe a person's life who is pure in heart.**

_____

_____

**Now describe your life. What does this tell you about the purity of your heart?** _____

_____

> "It is impossible to live pure lives until we have pure hearts. But if we have received a cleansed and pure heart from God, we are expected to live a pure life."

This heart purity is not produced by mental suggestion, by environment, or by education. It is a miracle wrought by God Himself. God says: "A new heart also will I give you, and a new spirit will I put within you; and I will take away the stony heart out of your flesh" (Ezekiel 36:26). Purity of heart is a result of a rebirth, a miracle, a new creation.

When we have properly confessed and renounced our sins and by faith received Christ into our hearts, then we receive a new heart from God. Only then can we be called "pure in heart." Only then can we know the secret of happiness! It is impossible to live pure lives until we have pure hearts. But if we have received a cleansed and pure heart from God, we are expected to live a pure life.

**Dr. Graham has emphasized our part and God's part in living a life of purity.**

**Label these parts as *G* for God's part, *O* for our part, and *N* for neither.**

____ confession of sin

____ faith to receive Christ

____ rebirth, a new creation

____ mental suggestion

____ a miracle

____ a new heart and spirit

____ a new environment

____ re-education

# Physical Cleanliness

God wants us *to be pure in body*. This includes physical cleanliness. There is absolutely no excuse for a Christian's being unclean, unkempt, or slovenly. If you have a pure heart, you will also want to have a pure body.

Physical cleanliness means more than just keeping our bodies washed, however. For example, God has given us our bodies, and we are to take care of them in every reasonable way we can. The apostle Paul commanded Christians to be pure in body and to take care of their bodies: "What? know ye not that your body is the temple of the Holy Ghost which is in you, which ye have of God, and ye are not your own? For ye are bought with a price: therefore glorify God in your body, and in your spirit, which are God's" (1 Corinthians 6:19-20).

We need to get proper exercise, and we need to eat properly. We need to realize also that there is a close relationship between our physical health and our spiritual, mental, and emotional outlook.

> "You shall love the Lord your God with all your heart, with all your soul, with all your mind, and with all your strength" (Mark 12:30, HCSB).

**Read Mark 12:30 in the margin. Give an example of how you can demonstrate love for God:**

- with all your heart (emotions):

- with all your soul:

- with all your mind:

- with all your strength:

# Moral Chastity

Being pure in body also includes chastity. Thus Paul says: "This is the will of God, even your sanctification, that ye should abstain from fornication" (1 Thessalonians 4:3).

How often the Scriptures warn against the sins of adultery and fornication. It is significant that in many references Paul mentions "uncleanness" immediately after "fornication."

Our newspapers are filled with stories of immorality in various parts of the nation. In fact, immorality is glorified today. Some of the most popular TV programs are about the decadent rich! The ideal of purity is scorned; immorality is laughed at in school—"God is old-fashioned!" What else can we expect but that thousands of our young people are growing up to be immoral?

**Make a list of times you hear sexual immorality condoned, advocated, or praised this week. Be sure to include references on television, in movies, in the newspaper, or on the radio. Include references where sexually immoral situations are depicted as normal and common.**

_____

_____

But the Scripture teaches that God hates immorality! One of the Ten Commandments says, "Thou shalt not commit adultery" (Exodus 20:14). Newspapers mention adultery, pornographic writers make it the theme of their writings, it is the theme of everyday gossip, children talk about it, and almost every magazine has discussions and pictures about it. This sin was so terrible that under Jewish law it was punishable by death. Under Roman law it was punishable by death. Under Greek law it was punishable by death. And under God's law, the Bible says, it is punishable by spiritual death. So why in the name of all that is just, proper, and holy should not preachers sound the warning against it? The Bible warns time after time that no immoral nation can survive and no immoral individual shall enter the kingdom of God. The Bible says we are to keep our bodies pure; we are to abstain from fleshly lust. This sin is a sin not only against the body but against God.

**Let your imagination run wild. A bill has just been introduced into the U.S. Senate making adultery a crime punishable by death. Write the first paragraph of a headline news story or TV news script. What is the reaction?**

# Pure in Our Minds

God also wants us *to be pure in mind*.

You can commit immorality by *evil imaginations*. In Genesis 6:5 we read: "And God saw that the wickedness of man was great in the earth, and that every imagination of the thoughts of his heart was only evil continually." God is concerned with our imaginations, for they in a large measure determine what kind of persons we are to be. Solomon said: "As [a man] thinketh in his heart, so is he" (Proverbs 23:7). If our thoughts are evil, then our acts will be evil. If our thoughts are godly, then our lives will be godly.

If God destroyed the world during Noah's time for its continual evil imaginations, is it not reasonable to believe that all of the sin, lust, and licentiousness rampant today grieve His heart just as it did in that day?

Many people dream of sin, imagine sin, and if granted the opportunity would indulge in sin. All they lack is the occasion to sin. So in the sight of God they are sinners as great as though they had actually committed immorality. All transgression begins with sinful thinking. We who have come to Christ for a pure heart, must guard against the pictures of lewdness and sensuality that Satan flashes upon the screens of our imaginations. We must select with care the books we read. I must choose discerningly the kind of entertainment I attend, the kind of associates with whom I mingle, and the kind of environment in which I place myself. I should no more allow sinful imaginations to accumulate in my mind and soul than I would let garbage collect in my living room.

> "Many people dream of sin, imagine sin, and if granted the opportunity would indulge in sin."

### Check the actions you have taken to create a purer environment for yourself and those you love:
- ❑ Write/boycott television advertisers
- ❑ Join organizations seeking to promote better television programming
- ❑ Use V-chip to screen television shows
- ❑ Use Internet filters
- ❑ Censor children's music, video games, CDs, DVDs
- ❑ Monitor closely what you/your family watch on TV or at the movies
- ❑ Switch channels as needed

# Pure in Our Actions

Not only does God want us to be pure in body and pure in mind, but He wants us *to be pure in conduct*.

Paul says, "Let no corrupt communication proceed out of your mouth, but that which is good to the use of edifying, that it may minister grace unto the hearers" (Ephesians 4:29). Cursing, telling smutty stories, smearing the good name of another, and referring irreverently to God and the Scriptures may be considered as coming under the expression corrupt speech. Our speech is to be clean, pure, and wholesome.

Under this rule of good conduct also come our associations. Paul says that evil companionships corrupt good morals (1 Corinthians 15:33). The Bible warns against being unequally yoked with unbelievers.

"Be ye not unequally yoked together with unbelievers" (2 Corinthians 6:14).

**To be pure in conduct and companions, I need to**
- ❑ watch the words I use
- ❑ be careful what I say about others
- ❑ choose different friends
- ❑ censor the jokes I hear and tell

The Bible teaches that purity of conduct includes truthfulness. We are also to be truthful in our business affairs. All misrepresentations of the quality of our merchandise, all false weights and measures, all padding of expense accounts, all forging of checks and other legal papers, and all unjust alterations of accounts are sins of untruthfulness and indicate lack of purity.

Being pure in conduct also includes honesty and integrity in dealing with our fellowmen. The "pure in heart" hearts are pure toward God and, as a result, are pure toward their fellowmen.

The greatest happiness that comes to the pure in heart is not only a proper relationship with others but a sublime relationship with God: "For they shall see God."

**Being pure in mind and actions does not appear to be of high value in our society. Place an X on the line to indicate the value you give these qualities.**

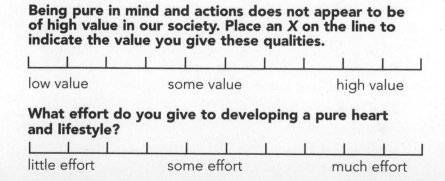

low value          some value          high value

**What effort do you give to developing a pure heart and lifestyle?**

little effort          some effort          much effort

Is Scripture memory a
part of your teaching
plan? If so, the beati-
tudes is an excellent
passage to learn. If not,
the beatitudes would
be a meaningful way to
begin this practice.

NOTES

## Before the Session

1. From print and Internet sources compile a list of popular movies,
   television shows, books, and music from the past 3-6 months.
   Bring 2-4 duplicate copies of the list to class, depending on the size
   of your group. Option: On posterboard arrange a collage of headlines and advertisements that represent our popular culture. Post
   the collage on a focal wall.
2. Have on hand tear sheets and markers.
3. Pre-enlist members to read the parable in Matthew 18:23-35.
   Select a narrator, the king, the servant, and the fellow servant.

## During the Session

1. Welcome participants. Share prayer requests and lead in prayer.
2. For those who may have joined this study in progress and as a
   review for others, recall Dr. Graham's statements about the beatitudes in his introduction in the first column of page 5. Ask the
   following questions: (1) *What are some synonyms for the word*
   happy? (2) *Do these beatitudes apply to everyone in every place and
   time?* (3) *Do you think Jesus' words were received much differently
   when He first said them than they are in our day?* (4) *What does our
   culture claim brings happiness?*
3. Ask members to open their Bibles to Matthew 5. Point out that the
   first and second beatitudes, "Blessed are the poor in spirit" and
   "Blessed are they that mourn," appear to be paradoxes. Ask: *How
   could spiritual poverty result in Christ's riches? How could mourning
   be a blessing (vs. 3-4)? Has it ever occurred to you that there is happiness in meekness (v. 5)?*
4. Ask someone to share a word of testimony about the blessings of
   hungering and thirsting after a right standing with God (v. 6).
5. Have members read aloud in unison verses 7-8. By consensus agree
   upon a definition of *mercy* and *purity.* On a focal wall print these
   definitions on a writing surface.
6. Form groups of 3-5 members. Give each team a blank tear sheet
   and a marker. Distribute the lists of popular media successes or
   call attention to the collage. Ask, *To what degree are the qualities*

*represented by the first six beatitudes admired or sought after in our society?* Ask groups to hang their tear sheets on the wall as a sign they are finished answering this question.

7. When groups have had opportunity to review each other's findings, point out that we are not called to reach a consensus on character qualities or become like fellow Christians. Our goal is to become Christ-like. Assign the following Scriptures that illustrate ways Jesus showed mercy and compare them with Dr. Graham's list in Day 2: (1) Matthew 9:20-22 (2) Luke 19:1-10 (3) John 4:7-10

8. Remind members that being merciful is necessary to receiving mercy. Introduce the reading of Matthew 18:23-35. After the reading, discuss the implications of this parable for our lives.

9. Have members turn to Day 3 as you review Dr. Graham's definition and description of the word *purity*. As a group, complete the learning activity at the end of Day 3.

10. Invite a volunteer to read Mark 12:30. Ask, *What is the relationship between physical cleanliness and moral cleanliness?* Allow for several responses. Emphasize that the mind, body, soul, and emotions cannot be separated. A human being is a person comprised of many parts. We are to honor God with every part of our being.

11. Depending on the age and lifestyles of your members, discuss the negatives of fornication and adultery that often are left untold by the media and advertising. Draw from the material under "Moral Chastity" in Day 4.

12. Say, *The modern myth is that thinking it is not the same as doing it.* Read Jesus' words in Matthew 5:27-29. Ask, *If we took these words literally, what effect would they have on advertising and fashion?*

13. Discuss with the class ways they might act individually or as a group to encourage purity in actions as well as in hearts and minds. Use the list printed in Day 5 and other suggestions to identify and address how society is bombarding us with promiscuous messages.

## After the Session

1. Read next week's content and complete the learning activities. Follow the suggestions in "Before the Session."

2. Pray for each member of your class by name. Pray especially for anyone who may be struggling in the area of purity.

# Peacemaking

day One

Blessed are the peacemakers: for they shall be call the children of God.                                                   Matthew 5:9

## The Search for Peace

The world is desperately searching for peace. There are millions of people who would gladly give their right arms to find it. They would like to have peace—deep, inward, satisfying peace.

They also yearn for peace in our world—freedom from conflict and war, freedom from the hatred and strife which divide families and communities, and freedom from fear of the future, wondering when a computer will malfunction or a maniacal dictator will place his finger on the nuclear or biochemical button and wipe out civilization as we know it.

"Depart from evil, and do good; Seek peace, and pursue it" (Psalm 34:14).

Jesus said: "Blessed are the peacemakers: for they shall be called the children of God." Notice, He calls for us to be peacemakers—not pacifists. There is a world of difference between the two!

**Pacifism has been defined as "peace at any cost." How would you explain the difference between *pacifism* and *peacemaking*?**

_____

Where does peacemaking begin? How can we become peacemakers? Peace can never come out of war. War is the sire of poverty, depression, suffering, and hatred—it has never given us permanent peace.

**Why doesn't winning a war necessarily bring peace?**

_____

**Think of a recent example to support your belief.**

_____

Where then does peacemaking begin? How can we become peace-makers in our broken, nervous, frightened, and dangerous world?

If we are to be peacemakers, we first must make our peace with God. The Bible says: "There is no peace, saith the Lord, unto the wicked" (Isaiah 48:22). The same prophet said: "The way of peace they know not; and there is no judgment in their goings: they have made them crooked paths: whosoever goeth therein shall not know peace" (Isaiah 59:8).

Man's conflict with man has been but an expression on the human level of his conflict against God. Until we find an armistice with God, we cannot know peace among ourselves.

**Read the four statements in the margin. Explain why we are at war with God before we become Christians.**

_____

**How does accepting Christ change our status from enemy to friend of God?** _____

Both ancient and modern men have discovered the peace of God. David said: "I will both lay me down in peace and sleep: for thou, Lord, only makest me dwell in safety" (Psalm 4:8).

## BECOMING PEACEMAKERS

To have *peace with* God and to have the *peace of* God is not enough. This vertical relationship must have a horizontal outworking, or our faith is in vain. Jesus said that we were to love the Lord with all our hearts and our neighbor as ourselves. This dual love for God and others is like the positive and negative poles of a battery—unless both connections are made, we have no power. A personal faith is normally useless unless it has a social application.

If we have peace with God and the peace of God, we will become peacemakers. We will not only be at peace with our neighbors, but we will be leading them to discover the source of true peace in Christ.

Christianity increases the scope and area of our lives. It takes us from self-centeredness to multi-centeredness. Conversion takes us from introversion to extroversion.

**Draw a cross in the margin. On the vertical beam, write the words *peace with God*. On the horizontal beam, write *peace with others*. If you do not have both beams, is the structure a cross?** ❏ yes ❏ no

*Is there any good reason why you cannot receive Jesus Christ right now? You must:*

*1. Admit your need (I am a sinner).*

*2. Be willing to turn from your sins (repent).*

*3. Believe that Jesus Christ died for you on the cross and rose from the grave.*

*4. Through prayer, invite Jesus Christ to come in and control your life. (Receive Him as Lord and Savior.)*

day Two

# Being Peacemakers in the Home

There are many areas of our lives where we can be peacemakers. There is no part of our lives that is not affected by this peace of God which we are to share with others.

FIRST: *We can be peacemakers in the home.*

In a complicated, mechanized age, it is no easy matter to keep the domestic life on an even keel. Modern gadgets, modern transportation, and modern social changes have all but revolutionized our domestic life. Families are fragmented. The old-fashioned taffy pulls, Sunday afternoon fun times, and family altars seem to have gone out with the horse and buggy.

Many homes today have become little more than dormitories, where the members of the family eat and sleep but otherwise have little communication with each other. One woman wrote to me and stated, "Our home is a war zone." Major newsmagazines carry stories of "latchkey kids," youngsters who come home from school to an empty house, seldom seeing their parents and growing up with little love or discipline. Our society has said, "Get ahead! Do your own thing! Don't worry about anyone else—run your own life!" But in the process family life disintegrates and children grow up emotionally scarred and insecure because they have never known the stability of a happy family.

The LORD will give strength unto his people; The LORD will bless his people with peace" (Psalm 29:11).

**Of the following stressors in family life, choose the top five in your household.**
- ❑ two-career family
- ❑ child(ren) in daycare
- ❑ staggered meal times
- ❑ conflict over chores
- ❑ financial pressures
- ❑ conflict over rules
- ❑ too many activities
- ❑ other? _____

**Of the five you chose, which could you begin to make progress toward de-stressing this week?   # ___**

The divorce rate has escalated drastically in recent decades. The home—which is the basic unit of our social structure—continues to disintegrate at an alarming rate, even among Christians. The breaking of the marriage vow is having an effect upon our other social institutions. A chain reaction has set in that could ultimately destroy the nation.

In the marriage ceremony, after the vows are said, the minister solemnly and reverently remarks: "What God hath joined together let no man put asunder." Is not God the party of the third part in a marriage? Should He not be taken into account in the marriage and in the home that emerges from that marriage? If God joins the couple together at the outset, should not His Presence be recognized in the home continually from that point on?

Many homes are in trouble today because God has been left out of the domestic picture. With the continual clash of personalities in a domestic pattern, there must be an integrating force, and the living God is that Force!

God can give love where there has been hate or indifference. He can make a husband sensitive to the needs of his wife, and the wife sensitive to the needs of her husband—instead of two people constantly clamoring and demanding only to have their own needs met. True self-giving love—the kind God has for us, and the kind He can give us for others—is like a beautiful diamond that sends out flashes of light from its many facets.

Many couples think that if they have a more luxurious home, get a better job, or live in a different neighborhood, their domestic life will be happier. No! The secret of domestic happiness is to let God, the party of the third part in the marriage contract, have His rightful place in the home. Make peace with Him, and then you can be a real peacemaker in your home.

In all of literature, the Bible gives the most profound and concise summary of love's facets: "Love is patient and kind; love is not jealous or boastful; it is not arrogant or rude. Love does not insist on its own way; it is not irritable or resentful; it does not rejoice at wrong, but rejoices in the right. Love bears all things, believes all things, hopes all things, endures all things" (1 Corinthians 13:4-7, RSV).

**In the margin, draw a triangle with God (G) at the top and Husband (H) and Wife (W) at either corner.**

**What happens to a couple's relationship with each other when they each move toward God? Write T (true) or F (false).**

____ 1. They grow farther apart.
____ 2. They grow closer together.
____ 3. They grow closer to God.

**According to Dr. Graham, what is God's "rightful" place in the home?** _____

_____

# day *Three*

# Peace and Our Community

SECOND: *We can be peacemakers in the community.*

Our society is shot through with slander, libel, and gossip. The strife in many communities is almost unbearable. Here again, the basic cause is a faulty relationship with God.

The Bible say, "The works of the flesh are . . . hatred, variance . . . wrath, strife, seditions . . . envyings" (Galatians 5:19-21). True, we find some of these in the first-century community of Christians. Yet "Behold, how they love one another" was the remark of those who observed the unique peace of the Christian society.

**Jesus told His followers to be in the world but not of the world. How does this teaching apply to being peacemakers in the community? Mark *A* (agree) or *D* (disagree).**

____ 1. We are to be cunning and wise; we don't want to be taken advantage of just because we're Christians.

____ 2. If I'm in a social setting where prominent citizens are gathered, I'm not going to stand out from the crowd by appearing to eat, drink, or do anything different from my hosts.

____ 3. I would represent diverse views in my community and thus would need to be open to different customs, beliefs, and morals.

____ 4. I would hope that wherever I go and whatever I do, I would stand out only because people around me would see Jesus in me.

How then can I be a peacemaker in my community?

The formula is simple: First, I must make my own peace with God, and then I can make peace in the community. The fruit of human nature is discord and bickering; "but the fruit of the Spirit is love, joy, peace, longsuffering, gentleness, goodness, faith, meekness, temperance" (Galatians 5:22-23).

Our trouble is that we have tried to build a good society without God. We have taken the Bible out of our schools and God out of our conversation. The result is that decency has disappeared from the community, and bedlam reigns. Peace and decorum will be restored when the individuals in the community give God His proper place once more.

That does not mean it is easy to solve the complex problems that face our communities. But they can be alleviated, and we must not withdraw or refuse to lend our hand in untangling some of the problems and injustices that bring havoc to some communities. Nor must we stand back and let those who peddle evil take over our communities and twist the minds and corrupt the bodies of our young people. Paul spent two years in Ephesus—and the corrupt practices of the magicians and others in that pagan city were reversed. We need more men and women who are willing—for Christ's sake—to become involved in political issues and concerns in their communities, and to be peacemakers in His Name.

"Great peace have they which love thy law: And nothing shall offend them" (Psalm 119:165).

**What would be the result if Christians removed themselves from:**
- school boards _____

- city councils _____

- parent/teacher organizations _____

In regard to racial peace, let me say that for true Christians there is no race problem! The ground is level at the cross and there are no second-rate citizens with God. Admittedly, the problems are great, and will not be solved overnight; but if all people concerned will make sure that they have made their peace with God, it will then be a simpler matter to make peace with each other. If we approach the problem with a vindictive, intolerant, and unchristian attitude, we are destined to failure and disaster.

**List one or more ways you have made a positive difference in racial relations in your community.**

_____

_____

# Peace in the Church

THIRD: *We can be peacemakers in the church.*

We might as well face it: Strife has even infiltrated our church life. It is true enough that the Church is now the Church militant. But as such its warfare ought to be that of dedication to revealed truth and divine holiness, and not internal bickering and carnal disputes.

**Would it surprise you to learn that conflict occurred in the early church? Read these passages and summarize the issues involved.**

Romans 16:17-18: _____

Titus 1:10-16: _____

Titus 3:9-11: _____

We read in the second chapter of Luke that Joseph and Mary lost Jesus one day. Where did they lose Him? They lost Him in the most unlikely place in all the world—in the temple. Strange, I know! But, I have seen many people lose Jesus right in church. I have seen them lose Him in a dispute about who was to be choir director, who was to play the organ, who was to be an elder, or who was to be the minister. Yes, because we are human, though Christian, it is easy to lose sight of Jesus right in the temple!

I know of two deacons who had quarreled over an old line fence, and they had not spoken to each other for a long time. One of them, wanting to make peace, took his Bible and went to visit his neighbor. Handing his Bible to his "old enemy," he said, "John you read and I'll pray. We must be friends."

But John, fumbling for his glasses, said, "But I can't read. I haven't my spectacles."

"Take mine," said his peace-loving neighbor.

After they had read the Word and prayed together, they arose and embraced each other. John handed back the spectacles to his neighbor and said through his tears, "Jim, that old line fence looks different through your glasses."

When we have the peace of God, we can see things through "the other man's glasses," and by doing that we can make peace.

# Working for Peace at Our Work

FOURTH: *We can be peacemakers at work.*

One of the greatest points of tension in our economy is the labor-management relationship. Many industries today are recognizing that disputation is costly on the part of both labor and management and are seeking industrial peace through God and faith in Him.

One minister wrote to us the other day and said that he was chaplain in three industrial plants in Indiana. The managers had found that if they sat down with their employees and listened to the Christian message once each day that everyone was in a better frame of mind.

In London, an industrialist gave his heart to Christ. He wrote to us that he now conducts a chapel service in his plant and that two hundred attend the service regularly. "Never has there been more peace in our factory," he wrote.

Would you like to be an industrial peacemaker? You can be one—whether manager or laborer—if you make your peace with God first, and then seek by His grace to impart this peace to others.

"Make it your ambition to lead a quiet life . . . and to work with your hands . . . so that your daily life may win the respect of outsiders" (1 Thessalonians 4:11-12, NIV).

**Consider ways you can have an influence in your workplace.**
1. **Organize a prayer or Bible study group before work, during the lunch hour, or after work. As long as you are not on company time, most employers will let you use their facilities.**
2. **Can you display Christian symbols or art work in your office or cubicle? Can you keep a Bible on your desk? If you don't know the answer to these questions, check the policy manual or ask your supervisor.**
3. **Use opportunities to give a word of comfort, praise, or testimony. "Let me pray for you." "Praise the Lord." "Let me tell you what God did." Be sensitive to co-workers and company policies, and if you are going to talk the talk, walk the walk!**

When an employer and employees really know Christ, the lie is given to the Marxist thesis that an opiate religion is for the common people. To know Christ is to have part in His saviorhood and Lordship of life. Godlier employers and godlier employees will find that the right makes a claim upon every life. Where the employer is Christ's servant and the employee is the employer's spiritual partner, they are linked in an eternal vocation.

# Peacemaking in Our World

FIFTH: *We need peacemakers on the international scene.*

Several years ago I was invited to Moscow to attend an international conference of religious leaders to discuss the subject of world peace. It had been called by Patriarch Pimen, the head of the Russian Orthodox Church. At first I was reluctant to go, knowing that my presence might be misunderstood or I might be accused of being naive or manipulated by Soviet authorities. But after much prayer and thought I went, and one reason was my recollection of Jesus' words: "Happy are the peacemakers." I went as an observer and also as a speaker, delivering an address to the entire conference on "The Biblical Meaning of Peace." Later a leading Western political figure told me, "At first I thought you were wrong to go. But you were right. We must take risks for peace, because the world is too dangerous unless we learn to listen and talk to each other."

As I made clear in Moscow, I am not a pacifist, nor am I for unilateral disarmament; nations have the right to defend themselves against aggressors. Nor am I naive about the very real problems and barriers that exist between nations of different ideologies. But we must do all we can to work for peace, in whatever ways are open to us.

Is it really possible, however, for a single individual to have any impact in a world that often seems out of control? Certainly! First, encourage those who are leaders to seek peace. Second, pray for peace. The Bible commands this in 1 Timothy 2:1-3.

"I exhort therefore, that, first of all, supplications, prayers, intercessions, and giving of thanks, be made for all men; for kings, and for all that are in authority; that we may lead a quiet and peaceable life in all godliness and honesty. For this is good and acceptable in the sight of God our Savior" (1 Timothy 2:1-3).

**The International Mission Board of the Southern Baptist Convention maintains a prayer line that gives specific world needs to pray about. Dial 1-800-395-PRAY (1-800-395-7729). (NOTE: Be sure to wait seven seconds until the TDD tones for the deaf have ceased.) Or visit the IMB website at www.imb.org. Then click the "PRAYING" button at the top of the page. From there you can "Pray by" countries, people groups, mega-cities, societal segments, and so forth.**

The only corrective measure in establishing peace is for all people as individuals to know the peace of God. Though I am not averse to movements that strive in one way or another for world peace, I have a strong conviction that such peace will never come unless there is a spiritual dynamic at the core. I pray for wars to cease just as I pray for crime to stop; but I know that the basic cause of both crime and war is the inherent sinfulness of human nature.

Peacemaking is a noble vocation. But you can no more make peace in your own strength than a mason can build a wall without a trowel, a carpenter build a house without a hammer, or an artist paint a picture without a brush. You must have the proper equipment. To be a peacemaker, you must know the Peace Giver. To make peace on earth, you must know the peace of heaven. You must know Him who "is our peace."

Jesus willed His followers something more valuable than gold, more enduring than vast landholdings, and more to be desired than palaces of marble—He willed us His peace. He said, "My peace I give unto you: not as the world giveth, give I unto you. Let not your heart be troubled, neither let it be afraid" (John 14:27).

Only as we know Him and the peace He imparts can we be peacemakers . . . and He promised happiness to a maker of peace!

**Notice that Jesus' promise is that peacemakers would be called "the children of God." Why do children worry less than adults? What is the spiritual lesson?**

_____

_____

The key is commitment to become peacemakers—to be men and women who actively seek to bring the peace of Christ to others and to our world.

## Before the Session

1. On a focal wall display an attractive grouping of pictures that show people at home, in the community, in the church, at work, and in international settings.

2. Optional: Make a visit to a Christian bookstore in your area and be prepared to make a report to the class concerning the variety of items that can be displayed in your home as reminders of your Christian heritage, such as wall plaques and pictures, knick knacks, quilted items, throw pillows, table decorations, and so on. Or, ask members to bring such items to class.

## During the Session

1. Welcome participants. Share prayer requests and lead in prayer.

2. Lead a discussion from Day 1 based on the following questions. Ask someone to write responses on a writing surface. (1) Who in our world today is searching for peace? (nations, organizations, special interest groups); (2) Who in our world today is disturbing the peace? (3) Who are the peacemakers? (4) Where, according to Dr. Graham, does peacemaking begin?

3. Invite volunteers to share testimonies of how they made their peace with God. Be prepared to share your testimony as an example and as a discussion starter. Refer to the steps listed in the margin of Day 1. If you have unsaved persons in your class, review the steps in detail.

4 Assign the following Scriptures to be read aloud: John 14:27; 16:33; Romans 5:1; 8:6; Ephesians 2:14. Ask, *What or who is the source of peace?*

5. Optional assignment to Steps 6-11: Form groups of two or more or make assignments to five individuals: How can we be peacemakers
   #1—at home?    #2—in the community?    #3—at church?
   #4—at work?    #5—in the world?

   Ask each group to report after 5-7 minutes and to include appropriate Scriptures as well as practical suggestions. After each group reports, discuss actions you will take as a class and follow up next week.

6. Ask members to turn in their books to Day 2. Invite volunteers to share ways they seek to keep God a priority in their homes. If you chose the optional activity, tell about the various items that can be displayed as ongoing reminders of your Christian roots, or allow members who brought such items to show them to the group and tell about them.

7. Conclude your review of Day 2 by asking, *What is God's rightful place in the home? What will occur if He has His rightful place?*

8. Review Day 3. Ask two individuals to debate the issue: Christians should be highly involved in political issues and concerns in their communities. One debater will take the pro (positive) side and the other will take the con (negative) side. Allow the debate to continue as long as productive arguments are being shared. Then, as a class, evaluate what was said, not the speakers.

9. Be cautious about discussing internal conflicts in your church as you look at the material under Day 4. Review the Bible passages and encourage each member to be a peacemaker and to regard dissension as a serious offense.

10. Consider practical ways members can be positive witnesses at their worksites. Allow several to talk about how ideas presented in Day 4 could be implemented in their workplaces.

11. Review Day 5, calling attention to the two ways Dr. Graham suggests that believers can have influence in a world that often seems out of control. Ask a volunteer to read 1 Timothy 2:1-3. Have members turn to Day 1 again and read the fourth paragraph of Dr. Graham's comments, the paragraph about war. Then ask, *Why doesn't winning a war necessarily bring peace?*

12. As individuals pray silently, guide the prayers by calling out, one by one, areas that need prayers for peace: the home, the community, the church, the workplace, the world.

## After the Session

1. Is there a follow-up action you need to take in regard to Step 5?

2. Read next week's content and complete the learning activities. Follow the suggestions in "Before the Session."

3. Pray for each member of your class by name. Include the prayer burdens shared during the group time.

# Persecution

day One

*Blessed are they which are persecuted for righteousness' sake:
for theirs is the kingdom of heaven.* Matthew 5:10

Who wants to be persecuted? We cannot see happiness in persecution.
No one enjoys being maligned. Almost all of us want the goodwill of our
neighbors, and it is difficult to see what blessedness there could be in the
enmity of others.

Offhand, it would seem that being a Christian should elicit the
admiration and acclaim of those about us. A Christian is usually one
who lives his life with kindness, honesty, and unselfishness. Such a
person should be blessed, not blasted, it would seem. His peers should
stand around him and sing, "For he's a jolly good fellow, which nobody
can deny!"

It would seem so! But such is not the case. And it is good that this
Beatitude gives us the occasion to sit down and rethink this age-old
question: "Why are good people persecuted?" Or as a modern-day
author has asked, "Why do bad things happen to good people?"

**Put a check by what you would consider persecution.
Put an X if you think it doesn't measure up to that
label.**

- ❑ taunting, mocking
- ❑ destruction of property
- ❑ discrimination
- ❑ exclusion from peer group
- ❑ losing presumed rights
- ❑ threats
- ❑ coarse, vulgar language
- ❑ imprisonment
- ❑ physical violence committed against you
- ❑ being sentenced to hard labor

# We Are Not Exempt

A Christian was released from a country that had a hostile regime. He eventually got a job working with Christians. He was asked one day how it had felt to be persecuted for his faith. With a surprised look he said, "We thought it was the normal Christian life."

You may have concluded, as have others, that there is usually something wrong with those who are persecuted for righteousness' sake, that there is some quirk in their disposition, some personality peculiarity or some religious fanaticism that causes others to mistreat them. No, that is not always, or let us say that is not usually, the case.

Nowhere does the Bible teach that Christians are to be exempt from the tribulations and natural disasters that come upon the world. The Bible does teach that the Christian can face tribulation, crisis, calamity, and personal suffering with a supernatural power that is not available to the person outside of Christ.

Christians can rejoice in the midst of persecution because they have eternity's values in view. When the pressures are on, Christians look beyond their present predicament to the glories of heaven. The thought of the future life with its prerogatives and joys helps to make the trials of the present seem light and transient, ". . . for theirs is the kingdom of heaven."

The International Day of Prayer for the Persecuted Church is November 9th. Visit www.persecuted-church.org and adopt a country or area to pray for each day from today through November 9th.

**If you were being persecuted, would the thought of heaven make your pain more bearable?**

❑ yes     ❑ probably     ❑ a little     ❑ not much

**How does your answer reflect your priorities?**

❑ heavenly focus with eternity's values
❑ earthly focus with material values

The early Christians were able to experience joy in their hearts in the midst of persecution. They counted suffering for Christ not as a burden or misfortune but as a great honor, as evidence that Christ counted them worthy to witness for Him through suffering. They never forgot what Christ Himself had gone through for their salvation, and to suffer for His Name's sake was regarded as a gift rather than a cross.

day *Two*

# Patience in Persecution

**North Korea**

In what was once a land of revival, where the capital city of Pyongyang was known as "the Jerusalem of the East," there are now believed to be more than 100,000 Christians in concentration camps, suffering for their faith as "political criminals," prisoners of conscience, suffering for their faith.

Since 1953 (the end of the Korean war, when the border between the North and South closed), some 300,000 Christians and more than 2,300 congregations and 700 pastors have simply "disappeared" from North Korea.

Record your reaction to these statistics below.

Christ told His disciples that they were not to count it a stroke of affliction when they were reviled and persecuted. Rather, they were to count it as a favor and a blessing. They were to "rejoice, and be exceeding glad" (Matthew 5:12). Just as Jesus had overcome the world, so they through His grace and strength would overcome the world. Thus they were to be of good cheer. Here is something to contemplate for those who are persecuted: When the godless plot, God laughs (Psalms 2:4; 37:12-13). When the godless prosper, don't fret (Psalm 37:7).

Christ's disciples were to be "more than conquerors" (Romans 8:37). They were to rejoice in tribulation (Romans 5:3). When beaten and threatened with worse treatment if they continued to preach Christ, Peter and John departed, "rejoicing that they were counted worthy to suffer dishonor for the name. And . . . they did not cease teaching and preaching Jesus as the Christ" (Acts 5:51-42, RSV).

As we read the book of Acts we soon realize that persecution and death intensified the joy of the early Christians. The apostle Paul could write, "With all our affliction, I am overjoyed" (2 Corinthians 7:4, RSV). In all his sufferings and sorrows Paul experienced a deep, abiding joy. He writes of being "sorrowful, yet always rejoicing" (2 Corinthians 6:10, RSV). With sincerity he declared that for Christ's sake he was "content with weaknesses, insults, hardships, persecutions, and calamities" (2 Corinthians 12:10, RSV).

I have found in my travels that those who keep heaven in view remain serene and cheerful in the darkest day. If the glories of heaven were more real to us, if we lived less for material things and more for things eternal and spiritual, we would be less easily disturbed by this present life.

In these days of darkness and upheaval and uncertainty, the trusting and forward-looking Christian remains optimistic and joyful, knowing that Christ someday must rule, and "if we endure, we shall also reign with him" (2 Timothy 2:12, RSV). As someone has said, "Patience *(hupomone)* is that quality of endurance that can reach the breaking point and not break."

At the same time I am equally certain that Christians who have spent years at hard labor or in exile, have passed through periods of discouragement—even despair. Those who have had loved ones destroyed have felt deep loss and intense suffering. Victory for such has not come easily or quickly. But eventually the peace of God does come and with it His joy.

Herein lies the fundamental reason for Christian persecution. Christ's righteousness is so revolutionary and so contradictory to man's manner of living that it invokes the enmity of the world.

**Describe how Christ has changed your life in ways that would make worldly people take notice.**

_____

_____

_____

day Three

# The Cross for Christians

**The cross believers have to bear has been mis-identified through the years. Be prepared to tell why the items below are not worthy explanations of what bearing the cross means.**

1. The premature loss of a loved one

2. Having to deal with a cantankerous relative

3. Financial or job loss

4. Loss of health, a debilitating illness, or an injury

5. Having to move away from close friends

Jesus said that a cross is the Christian's lot: "He that taketh not his cross, and followeth after me, is not worthy of me" (Matthew 10:38).

Does this mean that we are to wear a symbol of the cross around our necks or on the lapel of our coats? Or does it mean that we are literally to carry a wooden cross?

No! It means that the reproach of Christ's cross, which He carried when He was in the world, is ours to carry now. Being at "cross-purposes" with the world is part and parcel of the Christian life. We should not covet or expect the praise of ungodly men. On the contrary, we should expect their enmity. The very fact that they are inclined to persecute us is proof that we are "not of the world," that we are "in Christ." All of the persecution, all of the blasphemy, all of the railing that they would heap on Christ, they hurl against us. He took the reproach of the cross for us; now, it is ours to take for Him.

# The Privilege of Persecution

As Paul said: "God forbid that I should glory, save in the cross of our Lord Jesus Christ, by whom the world is crucified unto me, and I unto the world" (Galatians 6:14). This, Paul considered a privilege—the privilege of persecution. Paul gloried in persecution because in a small way he was allowed to share in the sufferings of Christ.

Now, let us remember that this Beatitude says: "Blessed are they which are persecuted for righteousness' sake . . . when men shall revile you, and persecute you, and shall say all manner of evil against you falsely . . ." (Matthew 5:10-11).

Many times we suffer because of our own poor judgment, stupidity, and blundering. There is no blessedness in this. I have known professed Christians who were dominated by bad dispositions, snap judgments, and poor manners and thought that people were opposed to them because of their "righteousness." It was not their goodness that people resented—it was their lack of it.

We must be careful not to behave offensively, preach offensively, and dress offensively, and, when people are offended and shun us, blame it on the "offense of the cross." Our personal offensiveness is no credit to the gospel we preach.

"We are pressured in every way but not crushed; we are perplexed but not in despair; we are persecuted but not abandoned; we are struck down but not destroyed. We always carry the death of Jesus in our body, so that the life of Jesus may also be revealed in our body. For we who live are always given over to death because of Jesus, so that Jesus' life may also be revealed in our mortal flesh" (2 Corinthians 4:8-11, HCSB).

**Herman is a long-time member of your church and a deacon. Herman makes up his mind quickly and cannot be talked out of his position regardless of the facts. He "proof-texts" the Bible to say what he wants at that moment. Herman often speaks of spiritual attacks when others oppose him. In the spirit of Matthew 18:16-17, you are part of a team that is on its way to Herman's house. What will you say? Write your thoughts in the margin.**

Jot down what you plan to say to Herman during your visit.

Shabby Christians are poor advertisements for Christianity. Paul said: "We . . . suffer reproach, because we trust in the living God . . . but be thou an example of the believers, in word, in conversation, in charity, in spirit, in faith, in purity" (1 Timothy 4:10,12). The reproach we experience is the natural resentment in the hearts of human beings toward all that is godly and righteous. This is the cross we are to bear. This is why Christians are often persecuted.

# Positive Thoughts on Persecution

Let us see what happiness and blessedness there are in persecution. As George MacDonald puts it, we become "hearty through hardship."

Our Lord instructs the persecuted to be happy. "Rejoice," He said, "and be exceeding glad: for great is your reward in heaven: for so persecuted they the prophets which were before you" (Matthew 5:12).

The word *joy* has all but disappeared from our current Christian vocabulary. One of the reasons is that we have thought that joy and happiness were found in comfort, ease, and luxury. James did not say, "Count it all joy when you fall into an easy chair," but he said, "Count it all joy when you fall into divers temptations" (James 1:2).

The persecuted are happy because they are being processed for heaven. Persecution is one of the natural consequences of living the Christian life. It is to the Christian what "growing pains" are to the growing child.

No pain, no development. No suffering, no glory. No struggle, no victory. No persecution, no reward!

The Bible says: "The God of all grace, who hath called us unto his eternal glory by Christ Jesus, after that ye have suffered a while, make you perfect, stablish, strengthen, settle you" (1 Peter 5:10).

Jesus, in the Sermon on the Mount, had some commandments for us with regard to our attitude toward persecution. We are to:

1. *Rejoice, and be exceeding glad (Matthew 5:12).*
2. *Love our enemies (5:44).*
3. *Bless them who curse us (5:44).*
4. *Do good to them who hate us (5:44).*
5. *Pray for them who despitefully use us and persecute us (5:44).*

I have a friend who lost his job, a fortune, his wife, and his home. But he tenaciously held to his faith—the only thing he had left. One day he stopped to watch some men doing stonework on a huge church. One of them was chiseling a triangular piece of stone.

"What are you going to do with that?" asked my friend.

The workman said, "See that little opening away up there near the spire? Well, I'm shaping this down here so it will fit in up there."

Tears filled my friend's eyes as he walked away, for it seemed that God had spoken through the workman to explain the ordeal through which he was passing, "I'm shaping you down here so you'll fit in up there."

After you have "suffered a while, make you perfect . . . settle you," echo the words from the Bible.

The persecuted for "righteousness' sake" are happy because they are identified with Christ. The enmity of the world is tangible proof that we are on the right side, that we are identified with our blessed Lord. He said that our stand for Him would arouse the wrath of the world. "And ye shall be hated of all men for my name's sake: but he that endureth to the end shall be saved" (Matthew 10:22).

**The old saying goes, If you don't have an enemy, you must not be doing much for Jesus. Using the chart on the top of the next page, assess your lifestyle. Would there be enough evidence to convict you of being a Christian? Check the appropriate evidence boxes.**

| Evidence | for the prosecution | for the defense |
|---|---|---|
| conversation | ☐ | ☐ |
| goals | ☐ | ☐ |
| desires | ☐ | ☐ |
| entertainment | ☐ | ☐ |
| magazines | ☐ | ☐ |
| wardrobe | ☐ | ☐ |
| leisure time | ☐ | ☐ |

**day Five**

# Maybe / Maybe Not

Sanders, the martyr, said, "Welcome the cross of Christ. . . . I feel no more pain in the fire than if I were on a bed of down."

Another martyr said, "The ringing of my chain hath been music in my ears; O what a comforter is a good conscience." Kissing the stake, he said, "I shall not lose my life but change it for better; instead of coals I shall have pearls."

You may not be called upon to suffer as the martyrs suffered, for this is an hour when Satan employs psychological warfare. Jesus said: "Men shall revile you . . . and shall say all manner of evil against you falsely, for my sake" (Matthew 5:11). The tongue often inflicts a more painful wound than does the sword. To be laughed at can be harder to take than to be flogged.

Some in reading this may feel that because they are not at present being persecuted, they are not living godly lives. That is not necessarily so. While there are countries where today to be an active Christian is to court death and worse, we live in a predominantly Christian country where active persecution is at a minimum.

Our environment, as well as the age in which we live, has much to do with the amount of persecution a Christian will be called upon to bear. I have known certain overly eager Christians who actually courted persecution for fear that otherwise they would not be living godly enough lives.

> "Never take one step out of the pathway of duty either to take a cross or to escape one."
> – Samuel Rutherford

> "Oh, to have a martyr's heart if not a martyr's crown!"
> – W. C. Burns of India

Remember, not all Christians are called upon to suffer at all times. Even our Lord increased in wisdom and knowledge and in favor with God and man. But the periods of popularity did not last. It ended on a cross. The important thing is to walk with Christ. Live for Christ! Have one consuming passion in life—to please Him! And let the chips fall where they may. I believe it was Samuel Rutherford who said, "Never take one step out of the pathway of duty either to take a cross or to escape one." W. C. Burns of India wrote, "Oh, to have a martyr's heart if not a martyr's crown!"

Popularity and adulation are far more dangerous for the Christian than persecution. It is easy when all goes smoothly to lose our sense of balance and our perspective. We must learn like Paul "how to abound" and "how to be abased." We must learn in "whatsoever state" we are "therewith to be content" (Philippians 4:11).

As we have said, the important thing is to walk with Christ, to live for Christ, and to have one consuming passion to please Him. Then, whatever happens, we know that He has permitted it to teach us some priceless lesson and to perfect us for His service. He will enrich our circumstances, be they pleasant or disagreeable, by the fact of His presence with us.

**Read John 10:1-15 and answer these questions.**

1. How and why does the thief enter the sheep pen?

    _____

2. How and why does the shepherd enter the sheep pen? _____

    _____

3. Why do the sheep follow the shepherd?_____

    _____

The tomorrows fill us with dread. John 10:4 says Jesus goes ahead of His sheep. Whatever awaits us is *encountered* first by Him—like the oriental shepherd always went ahead of his sheep—therefore any attack on sheep has to *deal first* with the shepherd—all the *tomorrows* of our lives have to pass Him before they get to us!

# Steps to the Abundant Life

In summing up the secret of happiness allow me to suggest several steps to living the abundant life:

- *We must recognize our spiritual poverty* (Revelation 3:17).
- *We must make sure we have received Christ* (John 1:12).
- *We must maintain a contrite spirit* (Psalm 51:17; 1 John 1:9).
- *We must be sensitive to the needs of others* (Romans 12:15).
- *We must not be "half-Christian"* (Matthew 6:24).
- *We must live surrendered lives* (Romans 6:16).
- *We must be filled with and controlled by the Spirit* (Ephesians 5:18).
- *We should seek for the fruit of the Spirit to be produced in our lives* (Galatians 5:22-23).
- *We must become grounded in the Bible* (Colossians 3:16). The Bible is our one sure guide in an unsure world.
- *We must witness for Christ* (Matthew 5:14,16).
- *We must practice the Presence of God* (Matthew 28:20). We should say or do nothing that we would not say or do in His Presence. But we must remember that He is not with us merely to judge or condemn us; He is near to comfort, protect, guide, encourage, strengthen, cleanse, and help.
- *We must learn the exercise of regular prayer* (Matthew 6:6; Luke 18:1; James 5:16).
- *We must develop a taste for spiritual things* (Matthew 5:6). Spiritual tastes, like physical tastes, can be cultivated.
- *We must not be critical of others* (Romans 12:3,10).
- *We must not be envious of others* (1 Corinthians 3:3; Galatians 5:26; James 3:14,16).
- *We should love everybody* (Romans 12:9).
- *We should stand courageously for the right* (Ephesians 6:13-17). Christ needs people who will take a strong, uncompromising stand for Him.
- *We should learn to relax in Christ* (Isaiah 26:3-4; 32:18).
- *We must not be excessively sensitive to what others think about us* (Luke 6:22-23; 1 Peter 3:16).
- *We must remember we are immortal and will live forever* (Matthew 5:12; 1 Thessalonians 4:17). As believers, we are to think and act within the framework of eternity. The sufferings of this present world are not worthy to be compared with the glory that shall be revealed hereafter.

"I am come that they might have life, and that they might have it more abundantly" (John 10:10 HCSB).

**87**

**leader Guide**

Since this is the last session of *The Secret of Happiness* by Dr. Billy Graham, plan your time so you can conclude and review this study as well as introduce the next study by Dr. Charles Swindoll.

NOTES

## Before the Session

1. Bring to class a world map or globe.
2. Collect data on the persecuted churches of the world. Include the Sudan, China, India, Nigeria, Indonesia, and most Muslim countries. Find out how Christians are being persecuted (killed, burned out of their homes and churches, or even taken into slavery). Visit www.persecutedchurch.org or locate other sources of information.
3. Make a copy of the three small group assignments in Step 8.

## During the Session

1. Welcome participants. Share prayer requests and lead in prayer. Discuss any follow-up action from the previous week's study.
2. Say, *In the twentieth century, more Christians around the world were persecuted than in any other century. We don't yet know if the twenty-first century will surpass these numbers, but it appears likely.*
3. On a world map or globe, pinpoint some of the major trouble spots where Christians are being persecuted. Relate the information you gleaned from the Internet and other sources to supplement class members' knowledge of world events.
4. Ask, *How does persecution take place in our country?* Then ask, *Why do we have so little persecution? Should we pray for more persecution?* Refer to Dr. Graham's answer to this question in Day 5.
5. Ask, *In Day 2 what does Dr. Graham say is the fundamental reason for Christian persecution?* Then ask, *In Day 3, how does he interpret the cross Christians are to carry?*
6. Enlist two persons to represent two contemporary Christians of the same country. Select one to represent a person who has endured a vast amount of persecution while the other has had almost none. Based only on this information and Dr. Graham's words in Day 4, put together a character profile of each individual. List the traits on a writing surface as they are named. Summarize the group's conclusions.
7. Ask, *Why in Day 5 did Dr. Graham say, "Popularity and adulation are far more dangerous for the Christian than persecution"?* Allow time for adequate discussion.

8. Emphasize that Jesus, as well as most New Testament writers, graciously endured persecution. Form three small groups of two or more and make the following assignment: From these verses summarize teachings concerning persecution.

    #1—Jesus:   Matthew 5:12,44; 10:22,38; John 15:18-20

    #2—Paul:   Romans 5:3; 8:36-37; 2 Corinthians 7:4-5; 12:10;
                   2 Timothy 2:3

    #3—Others: James 1:2; 5:10-11; 1 Peter 3:14-17; 5:10; 1 John 3:13

    Ask each group to report after 5-7 minutes and to include summations. After each group reports, discuss ways to respond in obedience to these teachings.

9. Conclude this discussion by framing appropriate verbal responses and/or actions that can be taken in situations we face at work or in other places where Christianity may be attacked or mocked.

10. Lead a review of this study of the Beatitudes in a manner appropriate to your class. Here are some suggestions: Ask if anyone can repeat the Beatitudes from memory. Read the Beatitudes aloud in unison. Read the Beatitudes aloud in rotation, one person at a time. Paraphrase or illustrate each Beatitude. Have learners recall a key thought from the study or say sentence prayers.

11. Remind members that next week they will begin *Living Above the Level of Mediocrity,* a study by Chuck Swindoll. Ask members to mark in the right margin of their books *a, b, c, d, e,* or *f* as you read these definitions of the word *mediocre.* The word *mediocre* means:

    a. in the middle      b. lukewarm         c. average

    d. a vegetable that can be boiled or fried in corn meal

    e. a type of media event or television program   f. other

    Announce that the answer will be revealed in next week's study.

12. Assign next week's lesson. Close with prayer, thanking God for the ministry of Billy Graham and for his insights into the Beatitudes.

## After the Session

1. Overview the six-week study of Dr. Swindoll's study, *Living Above the Level of Mediocrity*.

2. Read next week's content and complete the learning activities. Follow the suggestions in "Before the Session."

3. Pray for each member of your class by name. Include the prayer burdens that were shared in class.

*Charles R. Swindoll*

wrote the lessons for the Study Theme drawn from his book *Living Above the Level of Mediocrity*.

Dr. Swindoll is senior pastor of Stonebriar Community Church in Frisco, Texas, and chancellor of Dallas Theological Seminary. He is the author of a number of best-selling books. His radio ministry, "Insight for Living," is heard around the world on a daily basis.

## ABOUT THIS STUDY

In a favorite Peanuts cartoon, Lucy shouts, "Mediocre! Mediocre! Mediocre! Charlie Brown, you'll never be anything but mediocre." Charlie thinks for a moment and says, "Well, at least I won't be average."

**What does *mediocre* mean? Circle the words you think come closest to the definition.**

> in the middle          lukewarm                    average
>
> a vegetable that can be boiled or fried in corn meal
>
> a type of media event or television program

What does the word *mediocre* mean in a *Christian* context? Is the call to become Christlike a call to a level above mediocrity? Do you know Christians who seem content with just getting by in their spiritual lives? This six-week study will seek to motivate spiritual growth by re-issuing the call to commitment as we rediscover the Jesus who gave His all for us.

**If you could be one of the following, which would you choose to be:** ❏ a chicken   ❏ a vulture   ❏ a jay   ❏ a sparrow   ❏ an eagle   ❏ a mocking bird

In this study, you will be challenged to soar like an eagle in your Christian life.

# Living Above the Level of Mediocrity

Soaring in the Christian life. That's what these six lessons are about. Not grubbing for worms or scratching for bugs like a pen full of chickens, but soaring like a powerful eagle . . . living above the level of mediocrity, refusing to let the majority shape your standard. Being different on purpose. Aiming high.

Soaring isn't something that comes naturally, nor is it easy. But it can happen, believe me, I know. The ramifications of learning this have been life-changing for me. They include, for example, committing myself to excellence while many are comfortable with the mediocre, aiming high though most seem to prefer the boredom of aiming low, and marching to the distinct beat of another drummer while surrounded by a cacophony of persuasive sounds pleading for me to join their ranks.

Long enough has mediocrity called our cadence! Long enough have we taken our cues from those who ask, "Why be different?" or reason, "Let's do just enough to get by." Long enough have we settled for less than our best and convinced ourselves that quality and integrity and authenticity are negotiables. I'm convinced that achieving one's full potential is still a goal worth striving for—that excellence is still worth pursuing even if most yawn and a few sneer. And, yes, even if I should fail occasionally.

In the October 26th lesson we will learn that confronting mediocrity takes thinking clearly. The battle begins in our minds, but we also must choose which kingdom we will serve, how committed we will be, and to what degree we will express our devotion.

In the lessons for November 2nd and 9th we will tackle the challenge of living differently, focusing specifically on vision, determination, priorities, and accountability.

In the lessons for November 16th and 23rd we will examine four major enemies that need to be defeated: greed, traditionalism, apathetic indifference, and joyless selfishness.

In the final lesson on November 30th we will see that those who resist mediocrity must stand courageously when outnumbered, tested, discouraged, and tempted.

# Think Clearly

## It Starts in Your Mind

Confronting mediocrity takes thinking clearly. Everything we deal with in life begins in the mind, so we will begin there. We will discover the intensity of the battle that rages in our minds. We also will learn that those who confront mediocrity must do so through the perspective of another kingdom, ruled not by ourselves but by our Lord Himself— a surrender which costs dearly. It costs our commitment. And when that commitment expresses itself, it is revealed periodically in expressions of extravagant love.

### The Mind: Target of the Enemy

Let me get to the heart of the issue. The enemy of our souls has made the human mind the bull's-eye of his target. His most insidious and strategic moves are made upon the mind. By affecting the way we think, he is able to keep our lives on a mediocre level.

Read 2 Corinthians 4:3-4. Here we find the enemy (called "the god of this world") working in his favorite territory, the mind. Those who live in unbelief do so because he has "blinded the minds of the unbelieving." Most live their lives in spiritual blindness. It's as if a thick, dark veil were draped across their thinking to keep them from seeing the light. Only the power of Christ can penetrate that veil and bring light and hope and happiness. Paul describes this so vividly in verse 6.

Thankfully, there are those who turn from darkness to light. But don't think for a moment that the enemy relinquishes his long-held territory without a fight, a fight that endures throughout life!

### The Battle: An Insidious Strategy

Read 2 Corinthians 10:3-5. Even though Paul uses military words and ideas that suggest physical combat, it is imperative that we keep the right

"And even if our gospel is veiled, it is veiled to those who are perishing, in whose case the god of this world has blinded the minds of the unbelieving, that they might not see the light of the gospel of the glory of Christ, who is the image of God" (2 Corinthians 4:3-4).

"For God, who said, 'Light shall shine out of darkness,' is the One who has shone in our hearts to give the light of the knowledge of the glory of God in the face of Christ" (2 Corinthians 4:6).

perspective. Everything described in these verses occurs in the mind. What we find here is the strategy used against us to keep us ineffective and defeated—in other words, *mediocre.*

In ancient days cities were built within thick, massive walls. The wall provided a formidable barrier that protected the city, holding the enemy at bay. Before any alien force could expect to conquer a city, it first had to overcome that protective shield. Towers were even erected in strategic places within the wall. In times of battle, seasoned men with an understanding of military warfare would position themselves in these stations that towered above the surrounding wall. From these vantage points, they would be able to see the location of the advancing troops and shout their commands in hopes of counteracting the enemy attack.

For the enemy to take the city, three objectives had to be accomplished. First, the wall had to be scaled or penetrated. Second, the towers had to be invaded. Third, the men of military strategy had to be captured. Such was the strategy of first-century battles. In 2 Corinthians 10:3-5, we have this principle illustrated—not in a city, but in a mind.

Once the Lord breaks through the wall-like fortress and speculations, He encounters those "lofty things." Let's call these "lofty things" the mental blocks we've erected against spiritual viewpoints. You and I are prompted to go back to carnal habits when under pressure, when under attack, when undergoing a test, when doing without, when persecuted, when maligned, criticized, or done wrong. Our tendency is to rely on those traditional "lofty things"—those established thoughts that were passed on to us by our parents, our friends, and our colleagues.

And what is God's ultimate goal? Verse 5 tells us that it is to take "every thought captive." When He invades those lofty areas, His plan is to transform the old thoughts that defeat us into new thoughts that encourage us. He has to repattern our whole way of thinking. And He is engaged in doing that continually because old habits are so hard to break. Can you see now why those reactions you've had for dozens of years are still problem areas? Finally, you have some insight on your battle with lust, or envy, or pride, or jealousy, or extreme perfectionism, or a negative, critical spirit. And, more importantly, now you realize that there is hope beyond such mediocre mindsets. God's offer is nothing short of phenomenal! It is "taking every thought captive to the obedience of Christ."

"For though we walk in the flesh, we do not war according to the flesh, for the weapons of our warfare are not of the flesh, but divinely powerful for the destruction of fortresses. We are destroying speculations and every lofty thing raised up against the knowledge of God, and we are taking every thought captive to the obedience of Christ" (2 Corinthians 10:3-5).

**How does God get to His ultimate goal of taking all of our thoughts captive to Him? Number the following steps in the correct order.**

_____ overcomes mental blocks

_____ takes every thought captive

_____ breaks through speculations

## Conquering Mediocrity: A Mental Metamorphosis

Look up the word **metamorphosis** in a dictionary. Write the meaning here:

The essential question isn't difficult to state: *How?* How can I, a person who has absorbed so many years of mediocre thinking, change?

I have three words to offer—memorize, personalize, and analyze.

*Memorize.* In order for old defeating thoughts to be invaded, conquered, and replaced by new, victorious ones, a process of reconstruction must transpire. The best place I know to begin this process of mental cleansing is with the all-important discipline of memorizing Scripture.

*Personalize.* As you begin the process of replacing old, negative thoughts with new and encouraging ones, put yourself into the pages of the Bible. Use *I, me, my, mine* as you come across meaningful statements.

*Analyze.* Instead of continuing to tell yourself you are little more than a helpless victim, take charge! As soon as you catch yourself responding negatively or defensively, think—analyze the situation.

Those who break through the "mediocrity barrier" mentally visualize being on a higher plane. Then once they "see it," they begin to believe it and behave like it! People who soar are those who refuse to sit back, sigh, and wish things would change. They neither complain of their lot nor passively dream of some distant ship coming in. Rather, they visualize in their minds that they are not quitters; they will not allow life's circumstances to push them down and hold them under.

**Accept Dr. Swindoll's challenge to conquer mediocrity.**

1. *Memorize* a favorite Bible verse or passage. Be prepared to say it for your group when you feel ready.
2. *Personalize* your memory verse or another one by inserting your name in place of pronouns such as he, you, and anyone. Read or say your verse to your group with the substitutions inserted.
3. *Analyze* different ways to react to situations other than as "helpless victim." You will have opportunity in your group sessions to practice this skill.

day Two

# It Involves Another Kingdom

**Mark the following statements T (true) or F (false):**

\_\_\_ 1. God's kingdom is tangible, audible, and visible.

\_\_\_ 2. God's kingdom is a synonym for God's rule.

\_\_\_ 3. We choose whether or not to live under God's authority.

\_\_\_ 4. Whether we live under God's authority or not, we can experience true excellence.

\_\_\_ 5 A commitment to excellence leaves no excuse for mediocrity.

If we hope to demonstrate the level of excellence modeled by Jesus Christ, then we'll have to come to terms with which kingdom we are going to serve: the eternal kingdom our Lord represented and told us to seek (Matthew 6:33) or the temporal kingdom of today.

## Let's Understand What "Kingdom" Means

Before we press on in our pursuit of overcoming mediocrity, let's pause long enough to understand what I'm referring to when I mention the *kingdom*. It's one of those terms we like to use but seldom define. Part of our problem is that it is a tough thing to analyze.

> Write down your definition of "kingdom of God."

For example, while the kingdom is full of righteousness, peace, and joy, it isn't a physical, tangible thing. It isn't something we can touch or see. "For the kingdom of God is not eating and drinking, but righteousness and peace and joy in the Holy Spirit" (Romans 14:17).

Furthermore, this kingdom isn't verbal, something we can actually hear with our ears, even though it is powerful. "For the kingdom of God does not consist in words, but in power" (1 Corinthians 4:20).

If that isn't mysterious enough, I should add that while it is unshakable, it isn't visible either! "Therefore, since we receive a kingdom which cannot be shaken, let us show gratitude, by which we may offer to God an acceptable service with reverence and awe" (Hebrews 12:28).

How about that! We're supposed to seek something we cannot see, feel, or hear. And we're expected to embrace something that is intangible, inaudible, and invisible.

Enough tongue-twisting. Generally speaking, *God's kingdom is a synonym for God's rule.* Those who choose to live in His kingdom (though still very much alive on Planet Earth) choose to live under His authority.

So when I write of God's kingdom, I'm referring to His rightful authority over our lives. Only then can we experience true excellence.

What I want to communicate is that a life which soars is one that doesn't get caught in the trap of the temporal. People of excellence are those who see through the clutching greed of our times—people who have declared their undivided allegiance to Christ's message, a message that praises and exalts and honors the King of heaven, knowing He is able to humble those who walk in pride. Such a commitment represents authentic excellence, leaving no excuse for mediocrity. People who soar, that is, soar like God intended, are people who have humbled themselves to Christ's sovereign authority. They are citizens of His invisible kingdom.

day Three

## Kingdom Observations and Applications

Observation: *Kingdom authority diminishes the significance of all other powers.* The accompanying application is: *When facing the temptation to make a name for yourself, call on kingdom power.*

If you are greatly gifted, you may be able to do marvelous things that would cause the public to be swept up in your skills and in your abilities. In the process of your growing, you will find great temptation to make a name for yourself, to make a big splash, to gain attention, to get the glory, to strut around, to increase your fees, to demand your rights, and to expect kid-glove treatment. But instead, remember to call on kingdom power.

Observation: *Kingdom living involves many tribulations.* But the accompanying application reveals a source of strength: *When going through times of testing, count on kingdom endurance.*

Paul says that through many tribulations we must enter the kingdom of God (Acts 14:22). It's a rigorous statement and, without question, an unpopular one.

Now if you're in life only for yourself, you'll have no endurance. On that precarious top of the ladder, you'll always have to maintain your balance by maneuvering and manipulating, lying, deceiving, and scheming. But if you're committed to kingdom-related excellence, when you go through times of testing, you can count on kingdom endurance to get you through.

Observation: *Kingdom emphasis thins the ranks.* The accompanying application is: *When wondering why most people prefer mediocrity, realize the kingdom separates.*

Read Acts 19:8. Once Paul won a hearing in the synagogue in Corinth, he spoke openly for three months, "persuading" those who attended. About what? "The kingdom of God." I know that must have been hard for the Corinthians to hear because Luke uses the words *speaking out boldly, reasoning,* and *persuading.* The words *speaking out boldly* mean "to declare, as if making a proclamation." You can be sure that caught their attention. The next word *(reasoning)* carries with it the idea of "dialoguing." In fact, it's from the Greek term *dialegomai,* from which we get the word *dialogue.* It includes the thought of "pondering" and "disputing." One scholar renders it "debating." So Paul threw out to them thoughts of the kingdom, and then he entertained their disputes. Perhaps this same dialogue continued for three months as Paul tried to *persuade* them. The word *persuading* means "to prevail upon so as to bring about a change." And the result? Read verse 9: "some were becoming hardened and disobedient." See that word *hardened?* Interesting. It means "to dry." And it conveys the idea of being austere, stern, even severe. "They dried up" is the idea. Some were drying up with that message. They were hardened and disobedient. Kingdom truth does its own pruning.

> "And he entered the synagogue and continued speaking out boldly for three months, reasoning and persuading them about the kingdom of God" (Acts 19:8).

Observation: *Kingdom truth is central to the whole purpose of God.* The accompanying application is: *When coming to terms with the whole purpose of God, remember kingdom commitment.*

Read Paul's statement in Acts 20:20,27. What I want you to notice from these verses is that it is easy to shrink from the message that we have to tell if we are not careful.

If you say that you're the kind of Christian who wants to embrace excellence, who really wants the whole purpose of God, then you dare not leave out *kingdom commitment.*

> "I did not shrink from declaring to you anything that was profitable, and teaching you publicly and from house to house. . . . For I did not shrink from declaring to you the whole purpose of God" (Acts 20:20,27).

**Write a brief argument against the following statements:**

1. Kingdom authority brings with it popularity on the religious circuit. _____

   _____

2. Kingdom living means that God will keep you from harm and difficulty. _____

   _____

3. If you are faithful to the kingdom, you will draw large crowds of followers. _____

   _____

4. A kingdom spokesperson will tell just what people want to hear. _____

   _____

day *Four*

# It Costs Your Commitment

Some folks have the mistaken idea that Jesus deliberately tried to draw big crowds. It's true that large gatherings frequently followed Him during His three-plus years of earthly ministry, but never once did He attempt to generate a big audience. On the contrary, more than once He deliberately addressed certain issues that quickly diminished the number of onlookers. On one occasion, for instance, He pressed His points so stringently that many listeners walked away: "Many therefore of His disciples, when they heard this said, 'This is a difficult statement; who can listen to it?' . . . As a result of this many of His disciples withdrew, and were not walking with Him anymore" (John 6:60,66).

On another occasion, Jesus did a similar thing. Both times it was *commitment* that thinned the ranks. Let's take a closer look at what happened in that second encounter Jesus had with the growing crowds in Luke 14:25-33.

Here was a "great multitude" merely "going along" for the ride— a gigantic crowd of mediocre tirekickers, who were spectators, nothing more. It was a situation that prompted Jesus to look them squarely in the eye and confront their lack of commitment. Who wouldn't be stabbed awake by His thrice-repeated "You cannot be My disciple"? We're talking straight talk here! Jesus touches three nerves as He addresses the cost of commitment—*personal relationships, personal goals and desires,* and *personal possessions.*

## Personal Relationships

Jesus said, "If anyone comes to Me, and does not hate his own father and mother and wife and children and brothers and sisters, yes, and even his own life, he cannot be My disciple" (Luke 14:26).

When Jesus mentions that we're to "hate" father and mother, wife, children, and sister or brother, He doesn't suggest that we're to treat them maliciously and be ugly toward them. What He is doing is emphasizing the very real possibility of *competition in our loyalty* between Himself and those we love so dearly. Top-flight, uncompromising commitment to Christ mixed with the quality of life He expects of His followers leaves no room for competition. Outsiders who don't understand a Christian's commitment to put Christ first might observe such devotion to the Lord and misjudge it as hatred toward other relationships. It isn't hatred, but rather a matter of priorities—deciding who or what comes first.

What reaction do you have when you hear Jesus stated that His followers are to hate their fathers, mothers, brothers, and sisters? Record that reaction here:

**How would you be able to tell if you put your family before God in terms of your priorities? Check *God* or *family*.**

| God | Family | |
|---|---|---|
| ❑ | ❑ | Your mother wants you to come for Sunday dinner each week. In order to get to her house, you have to miss church. |
| ❑ | ❑ | Your daughter wants to take dance lessons. The only class that has space is during your adult choir practice. You feel a commitment to the choir and put off the dance lessons. |
| ❑ | ❑ | Your son wants to join a baseball league that practices three times a week and plays two games a week. |

In looking at your church schedule, all of the family would be missing some or all of their church activities. Dad says no to the baseball league. He and some other dads begin a Christian league for boys in the same predicament.

## Personal Goals and Desires

Again Jesus said, "Whoever does not carry his own cross and come after Me cannot be My disciple" (Luke 14:27).

Here the penetration of Jesus' words goes a level deeper as He refers to surrendering our personal goals and desires to His authority. Negatively speaking, it means saying a firm *no* to what you and I want and *yes* to what God wants. Already we can understand why many decided not to hang around any longer.

In the first century if anyone was seen "carrying his own cross," it was clear to everyone that he was on his way to die. Jesus uses that word picture to describe dying to our own personal pursuits and, instead, following Him fully.

## Personal Possessions

Finally Jesus said, "So therefore, no one of you can be My disciple who does not give up all his own possessions" (Luke 14:33).

Here again we see the accommodating language used so often by our Lord. He employs dramatic terms to communicate the intensity of His point. In today's vernacular, committed individuals live with shallow tent pegs. They may own things, but nothing owns them. They have come to terms with merchandise that has a price tag and opted for commitment to values that are priceless.

**Explain in your own words the statement, "They may own things, but nothing owns them."**

_____

_____

_____

_____

_____

# It Calls for Extravagant Love

At Passover Jews poured into Jerusalem from Galilee and Perea and regions beyond. Like a vast family reunion, thousands upon thousands filled the streets for days as they relived their historic deliverance from bondage in Egypt. But according to Mark 14:1-2 this particular year a few religious officials in high places were planning an execution. These men were putting the final touches on a plot that would lead to Jesus' death.

Suddenly, we are lifted from that scene in Jerusalem and transported a few miles away to a modest home in Bethany, where more than a dozen people are reclining around a table, relaxing and enjoying themselves.

Back then, a Jewish woman never reclined at a table full of men. And she certainly never let her hair down in public. She would prepare the meal and serve it to the men, but then she would back away to eat in another room. I mention that so you will be properly prepared for the shock of what occurred in verse 3.

Genuine nard was made from dried leaves of a rare Himalayan plant. And the particular vase Mary used, if it were like others used in that day to hold expensive contents, was itself a thing of beauty. Mary had a perfume so expensive that if you were to weigh its significance in dollars and cents you could have fed hundreds of families an entire meal. Over a year's wage was contained in that little vase (v. 5).

And without hesitation, Mary broke the vase and poured its entire contents over Jesus' head. Imagine the fragrance which swept across that room when Mary broke open the vase, and poured its contents down across Jesus' head. Then to the amazement of everyone except Jesus, she poured the last of the perfume across His feet, pulled down her hair, and then wiped His feet with her hair (John 12:3)

What an explosive act . . . what extravagance!

But not everyone loved it. The magnificence of the moment was marred by the murmur of some small-minded men (Mark 14:4).

Jesus not only defended Mary's action, He justified the woman on the basis of purity of motive and urgency of the hour (vv. 6-8).

"Now the feast of the Passover and Unleavened Bread was two days off; and the chief priests and the scribes were seeking how to seize Him by stealth, and kill Him; for they were saying, 'Not during the festival, lest there be a riot of the people'" (Mark 14:1-2).

"And while He was in Bethany at the home of Simon the leper, and reclining at table, there came a woman with an alabaster vial of costly perfume of pure nard; and she broke the vial and poured it over His head" (Mark 14:3).

"But some were indignantly remarking to one another, 'For what purpose has this perfume been wasted?'" (Mark 14:4).

Mary had her focus right. She wasn't enamored by the celebration of the season; she had not forgotten that her Lord's days were numbered. It was an "early embalming." How that changed the perspective!

Mary is one of those who chose to live above the level of mediocrity—one who truly soared like the eagles, a model of elegant excellence. Let me give you a new thought: *If you can explain it, it may not be extravagant enough!* Did you notice that Mary never once said a word explaining herself? She never said one word, not even when they rebuked her. How could she even begin to explain such extravagance? Mary simply did what her heart told her to do—without explanation.

It takes pure motive and a strong inner confidence to be that secure. Such extravagant love cannot be explained nor can it be justified to calculating, rigid, narrow minds. And because the majority will always be driven by what is practical, the majority will never understand.

When's the last time you broke a vase? When's the last time you did it and you were so secure you didn't even feel the need to explain it, though you were questioned and criticized? Believe me, those who soar will understand. Those who don't, I repeat, won't.

Do you at times act upon that impulse to abandon restraint? Do you ever have the courage to risk an extravagant expression of love? Then you're on your way to living above the level of mediocrity.

> "There's an old theatrical expression actors sometimes use in jest when a person is about to go out on the stage: 'Hey, break a leg.' I've got a new one for quality-minded, high-flying eagles when we greet one another: 'Hey, break a vase!'"
> — Chuck Swindoll

**In your opinion, what would be some extravagant expressions of love for God?** _____

_____

**Would you have opportunity to show love for God in any of these extravagant ways?**
❏ yes                    ❏ no

**Pray this prayer or write one of your own in the margin.**

Dear Lord,
I do love you, but I have not been very sacrificial in showing my love. I confess my selfishness and materialism. I repent of my desire for comfort and ease. As I continue this study, I pray that you will create in me the passion for excellence so that I may live above the level of mediocrity. Thank you for hearing my prayer. In Christ's name I pray. Amen.

## Before the Session

1. Make available a markerboard or tear sheets and markers
2. Bring a dictionary.
3. Have extra member books available for this new study. Bring name tags if you expect new additions to your group.

## During the Session

1. Welcome participants to this study. Introduce the author and study theme.
2. Ask, *Which part of you has the strongest influence on your actions: your thoughts, your heart (emotions), or your stomach (desires, pleasures)?* Allow several responses or a healthy debate.
3. Ask, *Why do you think Satan is interested in capturing our minds?* (Our thoughts, emotions, and desires all reside within our minds.) Assign three volunteers each to read one of the following: Acts 14:2; 2 Corinthians 4:4; and 11:3.
4. Optional: If you have a new believer in your class, ask him or her if there was a sense of having blinded eyes before becoming a Christian. Was the individual open to God's truth as a nonbeliever?
5. Invite someone to read 2 Corinthians 10:3-5 and explain God's ultimate goal when He breaks through our mental blocks. (taking every thought captive to the obedience of Christ)
6. Select another volunteer to read Romans 12:2 and explain how we can know the good, acceptable, and perfect will of God. Ask, *How do we renew our minds?* Call attention to the strategy Dr. Swindoll suggests at the conclusion of Day 1. (Day 1, second activity)
7. Appoint a recorder to write responses on a markerboard or tear sheet as you brainstorm the importance of memorizing Scripture. Here are some helps: (1) It helps us guard against sin (Psalm 119:11). (2) The truth sets us free (John 8:32). (3) What we put into our minds affects how we live (Colossians 3:5-6). (4) We don't always have access to our Bibles when we face spiritual attacks.
8. Make suggestions of Scriptures to memorize or have newer Christians work with more mature Christians to locate such

passages. Illustrate personalizing Scripture by reading John 15:5 or 16:33. Substitute your name for *you*. Allow several volunteers to find a verse and do the same. Then explain that we will return to analyzing later.

9. Review the answers to the true-false quiz at the start of Day 2. Invite responses to Dr. Swindoll's statement, "People who soar . . . are people who have humbled themselves to Christ's sovereign authority."

10. Ask volunteers to read their arguments against one or more of the statements in the learning activity at the end of Day 3. Lead a discussion of the implications of the statement, "Kingdom truth does its own pruning." (You may find yourself with fewer friends or less popularity if you speak the truth of God's message.)

11. Form three groups to each answer a part of the question, *From the material in Day 4, what are the implications for the cost of commitment: (1) in personal relationships, (2) in personal goals and desires, and (3) in personal possessions?*
When groups appear to have completed their tasks, call for reports.

12. Say, *At the end of Day 1 you were asked to analyze situations in which you might react in ways other than as a helpless victim. In Day 4 you were given true-to-life situations in which adults had to make decisions to place God above family.* Ask the small groups formed in Step 11 to think of other situations to pose to the class that present dilemmas families face. Allow time for the class to discuss possible solutions.

13. Invite someone to review the story of Jesus and the woman from Mark 14:1-4. Suggest members review their lists of extravagant gifts from the learning activity at the end of Day 5. Ask a volunteer to read the definition of *extravagant* from the dictionary. Point out that what one person may call extravagant may seem common to another. Explain that our willingness to sacrifice to demonstrate our love to God is more important than the cost of the gift.

14. Assign the lesson for November 2 to be completed by the next group session. Close with prayer.

### After the Session
1. Read next week's content and complete the learning activities. Follow the suggestions in "Before the Session."
2. Pray for each member of your class by name. Pray especially for anyone who may be struggling in the area of Christian priorities.

# Live Differently

Having come to terms with the importance of thinking clearly, we are ready to tackle the second challenge: *living differently.* Whoever clears away the mental fog is no longer satisfied drifting along with the masses. *Vision* replaces mental resistance. *Determination* marches in, overstepping laziness and indifference. And it's then that we begin to realize the value of *priorities,* a step which dictates the need for personal *accountability.* Each one of these stages precedes the next, forming a unit that spells out the basics of living differently—with excellence—in a world of sameness, boredom, and futility.

## Three Indisputable Facts about the World System

I have never read Matthew 6:24-34 without becoming aware of the difference between the way people *naturally* live (full of worry and anxiety) and the way our Lord planned for us to live (free of all that excess baggage). Then why? Why do we opt for a lifestyle that is the very antithesis of what He designed for us? Because the "system" sucks us in! We yield to a lesser lifestyle because "all those things the Gentiles eagerly seek" (v. 32) occupy our attention and ultimately dominate our lives. As I see it, there are three interrelated factors.

1. *We live in a negative, hostile world.* Face it, the system that surrounds us focuses on the negatives: what is wrong, not what is right; what is missing, not what is present; what is ugly, not what is beautiful; what is destructive, not what is constructive; what cannot be done, not what can be done; what hurts, not what helps; what we lack, not what we have. You question that? Pick up your local newspaper and read it through. See if the majority of the news isn't concerned with the negatives. It's contagious!

> "So don't worry, saying, 'What will we eat?' or 'What will we drink?' or 'What will we wear?' For the Gentiles eagerly seek all these things, and your heavenly Father knows that you need them"
> (Matthew 6:31-32, HCSB).

**105**

This negative mindset leads to incredible feelings of anxiety. Surround most people with enough negatives and I can guarantee the result: fear, resentment, and anger. Negative information plus hostile thinking equals anxiety. And yet Jesus said again and again, "Don't be anxious." The world system, I repeat, works directly against the life God planned for His people.

2. *We are engulfed in mediocrity and cynicism.* Without the motivation of divinely empowered insight and enthusiasm, people tend toward the "average," doing just enough to get by. Thus, the fallout from the system is mediocrity. The majority dictates the rules, and excitement is replaced with a shrug of the shoulders. Excellence is not only lost in the shuffle; whenever it rears its head, it is considered a threat.

3. *Most people choose not to live differently.* Those who take their cues from the system blend into the drab backdrop of the majority. Expressions like "Just go with the flow" and "Don't make waves" and "Who cares?" begin to gain a hearing.

Stop and think. In a world where all that cynicism is present, what is absent? Courage! That strong muscle of character that gives a nation its pride and gives a home its purpose and gives a person the will to excel is gone.

What then, does it take to live differently? Four specifics: vision, determination, priorities, and accountability.

> Look up the word *cynicism* in a dictionary. Write the definition for it here:

**Rate yourself on the following characteristics of a person who lives differently. 1 equals no difference and 5 equals much difference. Circle your response.**

I have the vision to focus on God's plan in spite of the obstacles.

| | | | | |
|---|---|---|---|---|
| 1 | 2 | 3 | 4 | 5 |

I am determined to follow God's plan no matter how long or whatever the cost.

| | | | | |
|---|---|---|---|---|
| 1 | 2 | 3 | 4 | 5 |

I set my priorities according to how they will positively impact my reaching God's goals for my life.

| | | | | |
|---|---|---|---|---|
| 1 | 2 | 3 | 4 | 5 |

I know I am accountable to God, myself, and others, and I take that responsibility seriously.

| | | | | |
|---|---|---|---|---|
| 1 | 2 | 3 | 4 | 5 |

## The Story of Two Courageous Men

Read Numbers 13 and recall the following five things.

*First, there had been an exodus.* The Israelites had been set free from Egyptian bondage. Pharaoh had let the people go. They had departed from Egypt with all their belongings and with all their family members.

*Second, under Moses' leadership God's chosen people had arrived at the edge of the Promised Land.* According to the last verse of chapter 12, "the people . . . camped in the wilderness of Paran," right at the edge of Canaan (the Promised Land).

*Third, the new territory was theirs to claim.* According to verse 2 God clearly promised His people the land. He told them in effect, "You'll have to invade it and fight, but I promise you that victory is *guaranteed*."

*Fourth, God commanded Moses to spy out the land.* In order to plan an intelligent battle strategy, Moses was to send in a few selected scouts to spy out the land.

*Fifth, the spies' assignment was clear.* Read verses 17-20. Once the spies found out those things their mission was accomplished! Never once did Moses say, "And when you return, advise us on whether we ought to invade the land." No, that wasn't their mandate. They were told to scope out the land, to do a quick, secret reconnaissance, and to come back with a report about what they had observed.

Verses 21-27 tell us the spies left and stayed gone for forty days. While these twelve men were in the land of Canaan, they took samples of the fruit and brought them back. Once the spies returned to the Israelite camp, they displayed the grapes. All the people gathered around and listened as the report was given. I'm sure there were a few oohs and aahs.

### NEGATIVE REPORT

But while everyone was getting excited, ten of the spies went on and added the words of verses 28-29,31. Notice in verses 32-33 how far these ten men went beyond their assignment.

"And the LORD spake unto Moses, saying, Send thou men, that they may search the land of Canaan, which I give unto the children of Israel. . . .

And they brought up an evil report of the land which they had searched unto the children of Israel" (Numbers 13:1-2a,32a).

"Then all the congregation lifted up their voices and cried, and the people wept that night. And all the sons of Israel grumbled against Moses and Aaron; and the whole congregation said to them, 'Would that we had died in the land of Egypt! Or would that we had died in this wilderness!' "
(Numbers 14:1-2, NASB)

Now what kind of impact did this narrow vision have on the people? Just in case you wonder if negativism and restrictive vision are contagious, read Numbers 14:1-2.

You say, "How could they ever say such a thing? God *promised* they would have the land!" Because negativism is infectious. Because lack of vision from the world system engulfs us. Human reasoning overrules faith! Natural thinking says you can't whip people that big. You can't win if you invade that land. I mean, look at how many there are! Count them!

You wonder what impact this report had on Moses and Aaron? Verse 5 states: "Then Moses and Aaron fell on their faces in the presence of all the assembly of the congregation of the sons of Israel." When the majority lack vision, their short-sightedness tends to take a severe toll on those trying to lead.

## POSITIVE REPORT . . . UNLIMITED VISION

Now the good news is that those ten spies were not the only ones who gave a report. I have purposely left out two courageous men until now. One is named *Caleb*. The other is named *Joshua*.

Both men ripped their garments when they saw Moses and Aaron on their faces and said, "Wait a minute! There's another side to all this. In fact, there is an issue at stake. It's time for us to be courageous. Let's start seeing this challenge through eyes of faith!" Read Numbers 14:7-9.

With vision there is no room to be frightened. No reason for intimidation. It's time to march forward! Let's be confident and positive! And after a Caleb-Joshua speech, people are ready to applaud and say, "Good job. Let's go!" Right? Wrong! Look for yourself: "But all the congregation said to stone them with stones" (v. 10).

### Why do you think mediocrity represents the majority opinion? (check one or more)

❏ 1. It takes less effort.

❏ 2. People feel comfortable around those who excel.

❏ 3. Mediocre is OK. Anything below it is unacceptable.

❏ 4. Determined people get too many bumps and bruises along the way.

❏ 5. Other? _____

# Vision: One Essential Quality for Excellence

Now, we are not studying ancient history. We're thinking about living today. My interest isn't in writing a book that traces the Hebrews from Paran into Canaan. I'm far more interested in helping people like us to cope with and conquer today's obstacles. And they are nonetheless formidable.

Did you observe something conspicuously absent from that story? The first thing that goes when you imbibe the system is courageous vision. *Vision*—the one essential ingredient for being an original in a day of copies gets lost, overwhelmed by the odds. We start focusing on the trouble. We start numbering the people. We start measuring their height and weighing them in. Then we start comparing the odds. The result is predictable. We become intimidated and wind up *defeated*.

What is your Canaan? What is your challenge? Which giants make you feel like a grasshopper when you face them? What does your future resemble when you measure it on the basis of facts and figures? You'd like not to surrender, right? You'd like to be courageous, wouldn't you? There is a way through, but you'll need one essential quality—*vision*.

*Vision* is the ability to see God's presence, to perceive God's power, to focus on God's plan in spite of the obstacles. When I think of *vision*, I have in mind the ability to see above and beyond the majority.

**Label the Bible characters in the following biblical passages *V* for *Visionary* or *B* for *Blind to God's Activity*.**

Ruth 1:15-18 ❑

Nehemiah 4:1-2 ❑

Daniel 1:8-19 ❑

Acts 24:24-27 ❑

# The A-B-C-D-E's of *Vision.*

Consider making a poster of "The A-B-C-D-E's of Vision" and posting it on your refrigerator. Read it every day this week and ask God to make you a Christian of vision—His vision.

A. *Attitude.* When you have vision it affects your attitude. Your attitude is optimistic rather than pessimistic. Your attitude stays positive rather than negative. Not foolishly positive, as though in fantasy, for you are reading God into your circumstances. So when a situation comes that cuts your feet out from under you, you don't throw up your arms and panic. You don't give up. Instead, you say, "Lord, this is Your moment. This is where You take charge. You're in this."

B. *Belief.* This is nothing more than having a strong belief in the power of God; having confidence in others around you who are in similar battles with you; and, yes, having confidence in yourself, by the grace of God. Refusing to give in to temptation, cynicism, and doubt. Not allowing yourself to become a jaded individual. Belief in oneself is terribly important.

C. *Capacity.* What I have in mind here is a willingness to be stretched. When God has you look at your Canaan with all its formidable foes, He says, in effect, "You must be willing to be stretched. You have to allow your capacity to be invaded by My power." Alleged "impossibilities" are opportunities for our capacities to be stretched.

D. *Determination.* Determination is hanging tough when the going gets rough. I have no magic wand to wave over your future and say, "All of a sudden everything is going to fall into place." Vision requires determination, a constant focus on God who is watching and smiling.

E. *Enthusiasm.* The word's Greek origin is *entheos,* "God in." It is the ability to see God in a situation, which makes the event exciting. And, by the way, do you know God *is* watching? Do you realize that? Something happens to our vision that is almost magical when we become convinced that God our heavenly Father is involved in our activities and is applauding them.

Even in a world that is negative and hostile. Even in a world where the majority says, "We can't," you can. Trust God today. With eyes of faith, get back in the game. Play it with great enthusiasm. Which is another way of saying it's time to live differently, which starts with seeing beyond the majority. *Vision* is the first of four specifics that will help us to live differently.

**Fill in the following acrostic with words that describe a person of vision. The first letter is completed for you already.**

V  <u>vital, virtuous</u>
I  <u>          </u>
S  <u>          </u>
I  <u>          </u>
O  <u>          </u>
N  <u>          </u>

day *Four*

# Determination: Deciding to Hang Tough

When I think of *determination,* I think of inner fortitude, strength of character—being disciplined to remain consistent, strong, and diligent regardless of the odds or the demands. I define *determination* as "deciding to hang tough, *regardless.*"

The thing that makes for greatness is determination, persisting in the right direction over the long haul, following your dream, staying at the task. Just as there is no such thing as instant failure, neither is there automatic or instant success. But success is the direct result of a process that is long, arduous, and often unappreciated by others. It also includes a willingness to sacrifice. But it pays off if you stay at the task.

Don't misunderstand. I have in mind being determined to accomplish what is right. I realize that criminal types could just as easily take this credo and commit themselves to a life of crime or some other irresponsible pursuit. But when the objective is good and the motive is pure, there is nothing more valuable in the pathway leading to success in *following one's dream* than persistence and determination. I know of no more valuable technique in the pursuit of successful living than sheer, dogged determination.

Who is the most determined Christian you know?

# Dream

There is another dimension to hanging tough we dare not miss. It is the thing that keeps you going with vision, the reason behind the determination. I call it a *dream*. I don't mean those things we experience at night while we're asleep. I mean a God-given idea, plan, agenda, or goal that leads to God-honoring results. People who soar like eagles, people who live above the drag of the mediocre, are people of dreams. They have God-given drive because they have received God-given dreams.

Most of us don't dream enough. If someone were to ask you, "What are your dreams for this year? What are your hopes, your agenda? What are you trusting God for?" could you give a specific answer? I don't have in mind just occupational objectives or goals for your family, although there's nothing wrong with those. But what about the kind of dreaming that results in character building, the kind that cultivates God's righteousness and God's rulership in your life?

Here are a few more ideas about dreams. Dreams are specific, not general. Dreams are personal, not public. God doesn't give anyone else my dreams on a public computer screen for others to read. He gives them to me personally. They're intimate images and ideas. Dreams can easily appear to others as extreme and illogical. If you share your dreams with the crowd, they'll probably laugh at you because you can't make logical sense out of them. Dreams are often accompanied by a strong desire to fulfill them. And they are always outside the realm of the expected. Sometimes they're downright shocking. They cause people to suck in their breath, to stand staring at you with their mouth open. A common response when you share a dream is, "You've gotta be kidding! Are you serious?"

One more thought on dreams: This is the stuff of which leaders are made. If you don't dream, your leadership is seriously limited.

*What are your dreams for this year? Make a short list in this margin.*

**Give examples of determined leaders who lived to see their dreams come true.**

_____

_____

_____

_____

_____

# Two Dreamers with Determination

Caleb and Joshua were among the twelve spies who went into the Promised Land on a reconnaissance mission. Forty days later the group returned with a divided opinion. Unlike the majority who panicked, these two brought back a good report. Ten said, "No way!" But these two disagreed. "We are well able. By all means, we should go up and possess the land." Now don't forget, Joshua and Caleb were surrounded by a majority of peers who were convinced the Israelite army could not do it. They were also facing a huge congregation of Hebrews who agreed, "It's impossible. Let's go back to Egypt." Yet in the midst of all those negative voices, these two men calmly stood their ground, "We can do it."

Now, I ask you, how can intelligent men look at the same scene so differently? The answer is not difficult: two had vision, determination, and dreams; the other ten did not. It's that simple.

That story is an illustration of life. We spend our years facing the very same dichotomy. To make things even more complicated, those who don't have vision or determination, and refuse to dream the impossible, are *always* in the majority. Therefore, they will always take the vote. They will always outshout and outnumber those who walk by faith and not by sight, those who are seeking the kingdom of God and His righteousness. Those who choose to live by sight will always outnumber those who live by faith.

Ten saw the problem; two saw the solution. Ten saw the obstacles; two saw the answers. Ten were impressed with the size of the men; two were impressed with the size of their God. Ten focused on what could not be accomplished; two focused on what could easily be accomplished by the power of God. Again, the persistence demonstrated by Caleb and Joshua is nothing short of remarkable.

Read Numbers 14:20-24. Caleb had "a different spirit." Was he some kind of superman? or genius? No, we never read such a thing here or elsewhere. He was simply a man with vision who dreamed great dreams

> Those who "refuse to dream the impossible, are *always* in the majority."
> —Charles Swindoll

**113**

and stuck by them. And as a result, God protected him and Joshua from death in the wilderness.

Read Numbers 14:30-35. I call that a serious judgment. God took all the people who had been a part of the original group that had voted to stone the leaders, and He said, "You'll die in the wilderness. It'll take forty years of wandering." Can you imagine the disappointment? They were right on the edge of the land of promise, yet they retreated and wandered, virtually in a circle, for the next forty years while the old generation of negative thinkers died off. Their corpses literally littered that region. And every tombstone was a reminder God means what He says.

Why weren't Caleb and Joshua numbered among the doomed? They had a different spirit. There was something about those two men that marked them as distinct.

Caleb and Joshua began well, but the real question is, Did those two eagles keep on soaring? We find our answer in the Book of Joshua. Read Joshua 14. By now the old generation had died off. Those who lived on invaded the land and fought their way to victory. Just as He had promised, God gave them the land. And now they're about to parcel it out to the tribes of the nation. When Caleb's turn comes, he stands tall and delivers one of the greatest speeches recorded in all the Bible in verses 7-12.

I love it! Caleb, though eighty-five years old, did not say, "Give me this rocking chair." No, not Caleb. He said, "Give me that mountain—up there where those giants live!" Caleb is *still* unafraid of the giants. The last thing we see of Caleb is his trudging up that mountain at eighty-five years old, rolling up his sleeves to take on the giants. Don't you love people like that—people who live above mediocrity? By now we understand the reason Caleb could do it, don't we? He had a dream. He had vision. He had determination. And age had nothing whatever to do with it.

Did Joshua end as well as Caleb? Was his determination still intact? Like Caleb, Joshua, too, delivered a great speech. Read Joshua's warning to the people in Joshua 23:6-7. After that, Joshua referred to his own family in 24:14-15. Yes, there is no doubt in anyone's mind that Joshua finished well. He was as strong in his convictions as he was in his earlier life. Since there is no way you can force righteousness out of anyone, Joshua chose rather to model it, to communicate it. He realized that a pursuit of godliness is something you have to leave with the will of each individual to make his or her own choice.

"Be very firm then, to keep and do all that is written in the book of the law of Moses, so that you may not turn aside from it to the right hand or to the left, in order that you may not associate with these nations, these which remain among you, or mention the name of their gods, or make anyone swear by them, or serve them, or bow down to them" (Joshua 23:6-7, NASB).

"Now, therefore, fear the LORD and serve Him in sincerity and truth; and put away the gods which your fathers served beyond the River and in Egypt, and serve the LORD. And if it is disagreeable in your sight to serve the LORD, choose for yourselves today whom you will serve: whether the gods which your fathers served which were beyond the River, or the gods of the Amorites in whose land you are living; but as for me and my house, we will serve the LORD" (Joshua 24:14-15, NASB).

**Pastor Michael wants to starts an after school mentoring program at the neighborhood elementary school down the street from his church. The naysayers have already pointed out the problems the church might face. He feels very much alone in this vision, yet he feels a strong leading from the Lord. What would you advise Pastor Michael to do?**

# Observations Worth Remembering

Three significant observations stand out as we come to the end of this account. First: *Age has little to do with achievement and nothing to do with commitment.* Both Joshua and Caleb were young men when they stood alone before their peers. Yet when they grew older they were still standing strong. Both men persisted in their convictions regardless of the passing years. Both men remained true even when they grew old. The ranks of humanity are full of those who *start* well. With determination and persistence, we can also *end* well.

Second: *A godly walk is basic to a positive life.* Joshua and Caleb kept repeating their full and firm commitment to the Lord their God. I believe that's a major reason they stayed so positive. Without a proper divine perspective, it is easy for negativism and cynicism to creep in. So if you want to maintain a positive, fulfilling life, you have to keep the Lord in the nucleus of your motivation.

Third: *Convictions are a matter of choice, not force.* Parents of growing, learning children keep this in mind. Remember there is nothing like the magnet of a model. You can shout and scream. You can discipline and punish and threaten. But there's nothing those kids will remember like the model you leave them. That will be cemented in their memory. You just live it, keep living it, and persist in your walk. That alone will be a magnet that will draw them.

**Four Nevers:**
- Never use age as an excuse.
- Never take your cues from the crowd.
- Never think your choices obligate anyone else.
- Never quit because someone disagrees with you.

**Did you notice the "Four Nevers" in the margin? Try to fill in the blanks without looking.**

Never use _____ as an excuse.

Never take your _____ from the _____.

Never think your _____ obligate anyone else.

Never _____ because someone _____ with you.

## leader Guide

### Before the Session

1. Optional: Bring grapes to illustrate the fruit of the Promised Land.
2. Pre-enlist three individuals to give reports in Step 6.
3. In Step 14 you have the choice of using the case study provided in Day 5 or writing one that might be more targeted to your class.

### During the Session

1. Welcome participants and open with prayer requests and prayer.
2. Review last week's lesson, which encouraged us to think clearly in order to live above the level of mediocrity. Ask someone to read Romans 12:2. Stress the importance of renewing our minds through daily prayer and Bible study, Christian friendships, and service through the church and into the community and world. Ask someone to define the word *kingdom*. Ask someone else to describe a kingdom citizen.
3. Say, *Today Dr. Swindoll is encouraging us not only to think clearly but to live differently. Living differently requires us to go against the way people naturally live.*
4. Form three groups. Ask each group to examine one of the three indisputable facts about the world system from Day 1. Group 1 should describe it; Group 2, identify the feelings it produces; and Group 3, give the common Christian response.
5. After the groups' reports, read the final two sentences of Day 1 that are located just above the interactive activity. Point out that today's lesson will concentrate on *vision* and *determination*.
6. Optional: Distribute grapes to be eaten while members hear the reports from the spies in Numbers 13. Ask four members to read aloud Numbers 13:1-3,17-25,26-29, and 30-33. Then introduce three individuals who will share their reactions to the spies report: an Israelite from the camp (Num. 14:1-4), Moses (Num. 14:5), and Joshua (Num.14:6-10).
7. Ask individuals to honestly examine which report—the ten spies or the two spies—they would most probably have applauded. Discuss the contagious nature of negativism and its debilitating effect on leaders.

---

If you have new class members for this second study of the quarter, ask them if they have any questions about the daily through the week study. Insure that they feel welcome.

NOTES

NOTES

8. On a writing surface, draw a vertical line to form two columns. Lead the group to contrast the way the ten spies and the two spies viewed God. As individuals answer, write responses in the appropriate column.

9. From Day 5 discuss the fate of all those involved in this historic event. Ask, *Why was determination essential for Moses, Joshua, and Caleb?*

10. Invite members to turn to Day 3 in their books. Read Dr. Swindoll's question, "What is your Canaan? What is your challenge?" Members may or may not feel comfortable sharing. If they do share, be sincere and courteous as this may be a sacred moment for them. You may choose to share your response to this question, or continue with a review of the definition of vision and "The A-B-C-D-E's of Vision."

11. Select a volunteer to identify the visionary Bible characters from the first learning activity in Day 3. Then ask another volunteer to fill in the acrostic for VISION. Ask, *Why do you think some people seem to naturally gravitate toward vision while others do not?*

12. From the learning activity in Day 4, ask volunteers to name leaders who lived to see their dreams come true. Ask: *What hurdles did they overcome? Did their success require determination?*

13. Review the "Observations Worth Remembering" from the final page of Day 5. Ask a volunteer to fill in without looking the missing words from the "Four Nevers" in the margin.

14. Optional: Read aloud the case study from the learning activity in Day 5 or choose the one you have written. Ask for several responses before a group consensus is formed.

15. Close with prayer, asking God to guide learners as they seek to take bold and courageous stands for Him as He leads them to follow Him.

## After the Session

1. Read next week's content and complete the learning activities. Follow the suggestions in "Before the Session."

2. Pray for each member of your class by name. Pray especially for anyone who may be a source of negativism in your church.

3. Does your class have a vision for its future? Do you need to be a pacesetter in dreaming about adults being saved and discipled, beginning a new class from your existing class, or taking on a new class ministry?

# Appraise Carefully

## Priorities:
## Determining What Comes First

Settling the issue of one's *priorities* is the third essential characteristic of those who live differently. *Priorities* have to do with choosing first things first—doing essential things in the order of importance, bypassing the incidentals.

**Can you name from last week's lesson the first two essentials of those who live differently?**

1. _____     2. _____

What is your greatest priority—honestly! Record your answer.

_____

### OUR TOP PRIORITY

We are forced to choose on the basis of first things first. We will never fly like an eagle in the Christian life until we are willing to determine who and what comes first. Life places before us hundreds of possibilities. Some are bad. Many are good. A few, the best. But each of us must decide, "What is my choice? What is my reason for living?" In other words, "What priority takes first place in my life?"

To be completely truthful with you, however, we aren't left with numerous possibilities. Jesus Himself gave us the top priority. We have looked at it several times already: "But seek first His kingdom and His righteousness; and all these things shall be added to you" (Matthew 6:33). Jesus said, in effect, "This is your priority; this comes first." He even uses the words "But seek *first*," meaning above and beyond everything else, pursue this *first*.

Before going any further, let's take a closer look at this command. The Greek word translated "seek" means "to search, to strive for, to desire strongly." The action is continuous—"keep on striving for, keep on searching after, keep on desiring."

Now look even closer and notice the objectives: The kingdom of God and the righteousness of God. Frankly, we don't even have to pray about our top priority. We just have to know what it is, then do it. If I am to seek first in my life God's kingdom and God's righteousness, then whatever else I do ought to relate to that goal: where I work, with whom I spend my time, the one I marry, or the decision to remain single. Every decision I make ought to be filtered through the Matthew 6:33 filter: where I put my money, where and how I spend my time, what I buy, what I sell, what I give away. That means a two-pronged question needs to be asked each time: Is it for His kingdom? Does it relate to His righteousness?

Why do I not even need to pray about my top priority?

_____

**List some actions that might not pass the filter test of Matthew 6:33 in the following categories:**
- What I eat _____
- What I watch _____
- How I treat my body _____

## A REMINDER OF UNSEEN VALUES

God's kingdom and His righteousness are unseen, you understand. We will never find His kingdom in tangible form on this earth in our lifetime. We will never hear the sounds of His kingdom or see Him ruling or hear the gavel in the hands of the Lord Jesus coming down in a court room where He sits as Judge. No, for the present time His kingdom is invisible, it is inaudible, it is eternal. So those of us who wish to soar above mediocrity in the Christian life have a commitment to His kingdom that forces us to press the whole of life through the filter of something invisible, inaudible, and eternal.

**How does God let you know when He is pleased with your priorities?** _____

**How does He let you know when He is displeased?**

_____

This filter (Matthew 6:33) helps me to conduct myself in terms of this top priority. Should I do this? Is it for God's kingdom? Is it for His righteousness? Should I respond this way? Will my decision uphold His righteousness? Believe me, that can get pretty exacting. Priorities are always tough things to determine. Furthermore, there are times we *think* we are on target, but we're not. If our hearts are right, God will graciously yet firmly overrule even the things we ask Him for.

# Are Your Priorities those of the Gentiles?

As I ponder Jesus' command, I notice that it begins with a contrast, "*But* seek first," the implication being that others are *not* seeking those things. But who are *they*? The preceding verse identifies them for us. They're called the Gentiles. In fact, look at what that verse says: "For all these things the Gentiles eagerly seek; for your heavenly Father knows that you need all these things" (Matthew 6:32). To identify "these things" we need to go all the way back to verse 24: "No one can serve two masters; for either he will hate the one and love the other, or he will hold to one and despise the other. You cannot serve God and mammon."

This helps us understand that "the Gentiles" are those who are trying to serve two masters. But Jesus makes no bones about it—"You cannot possibly serve both God and money." Be careful, now. He isn't saying it is impossible to excel and make money. The key word is *serve*. We cannot be a servant of both. Living out the kingdom life means that everything must remain before the throne and under the authority of the ruler. Everything must be held loosely.

I'll never forget a conversation I had with the late Corrie ten Boom. She said to me, in her broken English, "Chuck, I've learned that we must hold everything loosely, because when I grip it tightly, it hurts when the Father pries my fingers loose and takes it from me!"

What tangibles are you holding onto? What are you gripping tightly? Have they become your security? Are you a slave to some image? Some name you're trying to live up to? Some job? Some possession? Some person? Some goal or objective? (Nothing is wrong with having goals and objectives; but something is wrong when they have you in their grip.) Now let me give you a tip. If you cannot let it go, it's a priority to you. It is impossible to be a slave to things or people and at the same time be a faithful servant of God.

Now before we let this idea of "letting go" appear too stark, look again at the wonderful promise in verse 33. The latter half of it says, "all these things shall be added to you." How interesting! Remember verse 32— "these things the Gentile eagerly seek"? Well, now Jesus is saying "these things shall be added unto you." Those who seek them are off target. But those who seek Him are provided with whatever they need. When you think all that through, it just depends on where your priorities are. Isn't that a relief? Once you have given them to the Lord, who knows, He may turn right around and let you enjoy an abundance. Or He may keep them from you at a safe distance and just every once in a while let you enjoy a few. But they'll all be added to you from His hand rather than from your own.

**Recall a time when you got something through your own effort that you knew wasn't God's best for you. Describe what happened in the margin.**

> What is the one thing you would find hardest to turn over to the Lord? Record your response:
>
> _____

You have a good job? It's to be enjoyed for Him. You have a nice salary? It's to be enjoyed and invested for Him. You have good health? It is for Him. You have a family? The family members are for Him. You're planning a move? It's to be for Him. You're thinking about a career change? It needs to be for Him. That is true because He's the ruler of our kingdom. He is Lord. And that's not simply the title of a chorus Christians sing; it's a statement of faith. He has the right to take charge of our decisions so that He might be honored through them. Every day I live I must address that. Again, it is a matter of priorities.

Are you struggling right now between a decision that requires doing what is exactly right and losing closeness with an individual or giving in a little and keeping that friendship? You know the rest of the story. If Christ is going to have top priority, it must be according to the standard of His righteousness. There has to be credibility in what we do or it doesn't fall into the category of seeking His kingdom and His righteousness, does it? Why am I coming on so strong? Because He is to have *first place* in everything. Those who are really committed to excellence in the Christian life give Him top priority. Our choice of priorities determines at which level we soar. What is really first in your life?

**Number the following priorities with 1 for first. Add a category if needed. *Priority* does not mean time, or sleep might win. It does mean focus.**

____ family/family time/responsibilities
____ work—paid or volunteer—home or away
____ leisure/hobby/recreation
____ church/church activities
____ God/prayer/Bible study
____ other? _____

# Accountability:
# Answering Hard Questions

The fourth essential characteristic after *vision* and *determination* and *priorities* when it comes to living differently is *accountability.* People who really make an impact model this rare quality.

Did this paragraph frighten you when you read it? ⟶

Why? Analyze the reason for your reaction.

What do I mean by *accountability?* In the simplest terms, it is answering the hard questions. Accountability includes opening one's life to a few carefully selected, trusted, loyal confidants who speak the truth—who have the right to examine, to question, to appraise, and to give counsel.

Not much has been said or written about personal accountability in the Christian life. Practically every time I've spoken on the subject, I've had people say afterwards, "I never hear this addressed. I don't read much about it. In fact, I have seldom even used the word!" Because this concept has not been hammered out openly and often, the term itself seems strange. It can also be misused, since it is so easily misunderstood.

I do not have in mind some legalistic tribunal where victims are ripped apart with little concern for their feelings. There is too much of that going on already! Such savagery helps on one. It doesn't build up others nor encourage them to do better. And because many fear that accountability means only criticism, they resent even the mention of the word. I realize it is possible to clip people's wings so severely they will never soar in the Christian life. But trust me, that's the farthest thought from my mind when I write of accountability.

**How would you describe the concept of accountability to someone who has never heard the term before? (underline one or more)**

| | | |
|---|---|---|
| confrontation | truthfulness | sounding board |
| rebuke | appraisal | perspective |
| counsel | backbiting | advice |

## FOUR QUALITIES IN ACCOUNTABILITY

People who are accountable usually have four qualities:

• *Vulnerability*—capable of being wounded, shown to be wrong, even admitting it before being confronted.

• *Teachability*—a willingness to learn, being quick to hear and respond to reproof, being open to counsel.

• *Availability*—accessible, touchable, able to be interrupted.

• *Honesty*—committed to the truth regardless of how much it hurts, a willingness to admit the truth no matter how difficult or humiliating the admission may be. Hating all that is phony or false.

I am more than ever aware of why accountability is resisted by the majority. Those with fragile egos can't handle it. And prima donna types won't tolerate it. They have a greater desire to look good and make a stunning impression than anything else. I mean, "the very idea of some- one probing into my life!"

Again, don't misunderstand. I'm not suggesting for a moment that accountability gives the general public carte blanche access to any and all areas of one's private life. I referred to a few carefully selected, trusted, loyal confidants. They are the ones who have earned the right to come alongside and, when it seems appropriate and necessary, ask the hard questions. The purpose of the relationship is not to make someone squirm or to pull rank and devastate an individual; no, not at all. Rather, it is to be a helpful sounding board, to guard someone from potential peril, to identify the possibility of a "blind spot," to serve in an advisory capacity, bringing perspective and wisdom where such may be lacking.

"In our society a lack of accountability is considered the norm."
—Charles Swindoll

**Have you had a "blind spot" identified by a friend, spouse, or teacher?**
❏ no     ❏ yes

**Did that information make a positive difference in your life? If so, tell how.** _____
_____

In our society a lack of accountability is considered the norm. This is true despite the fact that *un*accountability is both unwise and unbiblical, not to mention downright perilous!

# day *Four*

# Scriptural Analysis of Accountability

I find three major *biblical principles* in support of accountability.

1. *Accountability to God is inescapable and inevitable.*

Read Matthew 12:35-36. No one knows precisely how that "accounting" will transpire. Many have guessed, some have assumed, but no one knows the details of the process. We are simply told that there will be a day when we will give an account of ourselves before our God. It is inescapable, and it is inevitable.

Read Romans 14:10-12. I call that straight and to the point. What else can be said? God's Book teaches that a future, individualized accountability to God is both inescapable and inevitable.

2. *Accountability to spiritual leaders is commanded by God and is profitable to us.* Most folks have no argument with being accountable to God. He is our Father; He is perfect. He has every right to hear about our lives. He is able to judge us without preconceived ideas or prejudices. But the rub occurs when we think about giving an account to *anyone* on earth. This is especially true among those who are independent-minded, self-made men and women and certainly those who have been burned by spiritual leaders in the past.

In the Book of Hebrews we read, "Obey your leaders, and submit to them; for they keep watch over your souls, as those who will give an account. Let them do this with joy and not with grief, for this would be unprofitable for you (Hebrews 13:17).

Spiritual leaders have been given, among other responsibilities, the difficult assignment of keeping "watch over your souls." And not only that, but we are told it is profitable for us to be accountable to them. Not one of us is an island. We need one another. Sometimes we need to hear another's reproof.

"The good man out of his good treasure brings forth what is good; and the evil man out of his evil treasure brings forth what is evil. And I say to you, that every careless word that men shall speak, they shall render account for it in the day of judgment" (Matthew 12:35-36).

"But you, why do you judge your brother? Or you again, why do you regard your brother with contempt? For we shall all stand before the judgment seat of God. For it is written, 'AS I LIVE, SAYS THE LORD, EVERY KNEE SHALL BOW TO ME, AND EVERY TONGUE SHALL GIVE PRAISE TO GOD.' So then each one of us shall give account of himself to God" (Romans 14:10-12).

**Check some ways your pastor keeps watch over your soul.**

- ❑ I call his office with prayer requests for my family and others.
- ❑ I ask for his prayers when I am facing spiritual battles or temptations.
- ❑ I seek his counsel when I am confronted with difficult decisions.
- ❑ I regularly attend worship services and Bible studies led by the pastor.
- ❑ Other? _____

**If your pastor is not watching over your soul, who is?**

_____

Believe me, if you think it is tough to *hear* such reproof, try giving it! Few assignments are more difficult for a spiritual leader. If one has the courage to call you into account and does it in the right way, with the right motive, be humble enough to accept the confrontation. Understand that it was terribly difficult to work up the courage to say anything in the first place. And know that that person has the good of the church at heart, not some private vendetta. In the long run, your commitment to excellence will be enhanced, and you will be able to soar higher in the Christian life.

3. *Accountability to one another is helpful and healthy.* This process is not limited to spiritual leaders, however. We need it on a personal level as well.

Take the time to read and digest Romans 12:9-16; 15:1-2,14; Galatians 5:25–6:2. Read each word. Linger long enough to absorb the truth. And try hard not to be defensive.

I repeat, there must be accountability! We have it with our teachers at school, our bosses at work, our coaches on the team, the banks that hold the mortgages on our homes, and the cop on the corner. Strangely, somehow we don't feel the need to cultivate accountability on a personal level. The home is an ideal place to learn how to be accountable.

**What are some practical, helpful ways spouses or roommates can hold each other accountable:**

- in the kitchen _____
- in the bathroom _____
- in the laundry room _____

# Practical Advantages of Personal Appraisal

I can think of at least three practical advantages of accountability—all based on statements found in the ancient Books of Proverbs and Psalms.

First advantage: *When we are regularly accountable, we're less likely to stumble into a trap.* Other eyes, more perceptive and objective than ours, can see traps that we may fail to detect. Read Proverbs 13:10,14,18,20 and 15:31-33.

Now for the second advantage of accountability: *When we are regularly accountable, we are more likely to see the whole picture.* When we have a sounding board, an accountable partner or group who traffics in truth, we're more likely to see the whole picture. I notice that my life tends to get quite narrow if my world is reduced to my own perspective—just a restricted, tight radius. But with the counsel of a friend, my world expands. I become more aware; I gain depth and I discover innuendo and I find another vista or dimension I would have missed all alone with my two-by-four mind. "Iron sharpens iron, so one man sharpens another" (Proverbs 27:17).

The third advantage of accountability: *When we are regularly accountable, we are not likely to get away with sinful and unwise actions.* "Faithful are the wounds of a friend, but deceitful are the kisses of an enemy" (Proverbs 27:6).

## AN HONEST EVALUATION OF OURSELVES

Can you list three additional practical advantages of accountability?

1. _____
2. _____
3. _____

Instead of wishing someone else were reading this, let's play like it's just the two of us. I have the privilege of writing about something that is very, very personal to you—*your* life, *your* private world. To make it palatable, allow me to ask you a few questions. I would like you simply to answer them "Yes" or "No." They are hard questions, I warn you. And you may be embarrassed if someone saw your answers, perhaps, because you wouldn't be able to explain them fully. So just think your answer, okay?

Question 1. *Can you name one or more people outside your family to whom you have made yourself regularly accountable?* And before you answer, this is what I mean. That person has quick and easy access to your life. He (or she) is free to ask you things like "What's going on?" and "Why?" This person wouldn't hesitate to probe if he were concerned about something you were doing that seemed unwise or hurtful. This friend usually knows your whereabouts and can regularly vouch for your motives. He or she has your private phone number. He isn't afraid to interrupt you. There's a well-developed love connection between you. You've helped cultivate it. Do you have at least one person like that, preferably two or three?

If your answer is "No," rather than just stopping here with a deep sigh, thinking, *I'm out of luck,* take this as a challenge. Say to yourself, "I need to search for someone, a person who I know will take that kind of time with me. And I'm going to invite that person to begin a friendship. We're going to have a meal or two together, and we're going to get to know each other, and I'm going to see if perhaps this is the one to whom I should open my life." I plead with you, don't put it off.

**Before we become too judgmental about our friends, let's ask ourselves these questions.**

1. Am I the kind of friend I would choose for an accountability partner? ❑ yes ❑ no
2. Do I keep secrets? Are confidences safe with me? ❑ yes ❑ no
3. Do I exercise tact when sharing a word of rebuke or criticism? ❑ yes ❑ no
4. Am I a reflective listener? Would I allow the other person to talk without continually jumping into the conversation to give my opinion? ❑ yes ❑ no
5. Would I make time available if I felt my friend might receive more than (s)he gave? ❑ yes ❑ no

Question 2. *Are you aware of the dangers of unaccountability?* Again, before you answer, I'm talking about dangers like unattractive blind spots, unhealthy relationships, unchecked habits, unspoken motives that will never be known without such a friend. Are you aware of where these dangers will lead if unaccountability continues? Be honest now. Ponder the consequences of an unaccountable life.

Maybe you have to admit that you've been far too proud, lived much too secretly. When I decided to let down my guard, I wrote out this simple prayer to God. It helped break down my resistance to the counsel of others.

In the margin below, write your prayer to God asking Him to help you break down your resistance to counsel from other believers.

> Lord, I am willing
> To receive what You give
> To lack what You withhold
> To relinquish what You take
> To suffer what You inflict
> To be what You require.
> And, Lord, if others are to be
> Your messengers to me,
> I am willing to hear and heed
> What they have to say. Amen.

Question 3. *When was the last time you gave an account for the "private areas" of your life to someone outside your family?* Like your finances, sizable purchases, or your pattern for giving? Does anyone know how much (or how little) you give? Does anyone give you counsel of what seems wise and what seems a bit irresponsible in the use of your money? Has someone ever talked to you about sacrificing in the realm of finances? They won't without your invitation.

How about occupational diligence? Does anyone know how much or how little time you really spend at the office? Is anybody aware of the attitude you have there, so that he or she is able to help you see its impact on the lives of others? Maybe someone needs to say you're working *too many* hours. Does someone have a right to that secret world of yours?

How about a schedule of activities? Have you had anyone pull up to you recently and say, "You know you're just too busy. You're away from home too many hours. Why do you say yes so often?" You may be approaching "burnout" without realizing it.

How about addressing your lust? Does anybody know how much you struggle with pornography? Anyone know what you check out at the video stores, or which magazines you linger over? How about a level of entertainment that you've decided you can get away with because nobody knows?

If you do not have an accountability partner or group, list the actions you will take to establish one.

1. _____
2. _____
3. _____

Those heroes who soar high above the level of mediocrity in the Christian life possess vision, apply determination, and maintain priorities. But how is it they keep from danger and do not suffer a fall from those heights? By now you know the secret. Accountability— they don't avoid the hard questions.

**leader Guide**

## Before the Session

1. Optional: Invite your pastor or associate pastor to class to discuss how he keeps watch over the souls of church members (Hebrews 13:17). (See Day 4.) Tell him how long and what time you want him to speak. When he enters the room, move quickly to Step 12. After he leaves, resume the lesson plan where you were when he arrived.

2. Print Matthew 6:33 on a tear sheet. Fold it so that it can't be read and hang it on a focal wall.

## During the Session

1. Welcome participants and open with prayer requests and prayer.

2. Review last week's lesson, which encouraged us to live differently in order to live above the level of mediocrity in the Christian life. Ask someone to describe the two qualities we must have in order to overcome the hurdles of negativism. (vision and determination)

3. Say, *Today Dr. Swindoll gives us two additional characteristics necessary for living differently.* Ask, *Who can name them?* (priorities and accountability)

4. Unfold the tear sheet on which you have written Matthew 6:33. Ask three teams of two to explain the meaning of (a) seek; (b) kingdom; (c) righteousness. Ask the remainder of the class to be prepared to discuss the last half of the verse.

5. After the groups' report, summarize the importance of determining who is really first in your life. Invite volunteers to share their responses to the learning activity at the end of Day 1.

6. Ask, *What does it mean to "hold everything loosely"?* (Day 2) Invite volunteers to recall a time when they got something through their own efforts that they knew wasn't God priority for them. Ask them to tell what happened. Share an experience of your own as a discussion starter.

7. Ask volunteers to share an example of someone from their past who was a good role model for setting and keeping priorities. Point out that living a disciplined life is often not popular with an "I want it now" generation. That's why vision and determination must be a weapon in the arsenal of those who set priorities.

If you feel led to promote accountability groups in your church, remember that they require a high level of trust level and confidentiality.

NOTES

8. Ask members to turn to Day 3. With someone acting as recorder, ask them to brainstorm words they associate with accountability. Then, review the list to see how many of the words have positive connotations.

9. Ask: *Why might the word* accountable *have a negative association? How can we encourage a more positive image of the word for ourselves and others?*

10. Review the four qualities which Dr. Swindoll identifies as characteristics of people who are accountable (Day 3). Ask members to *underline* the qualities that would be the most difficult for them and to *circle* those that would feel natural.

11. Ask one volunteer to explain why accountability is important for a Christian. Then ask another individual to explain why unaccountability is both unwise and possibly perilous.

12. Optional: Introduce the pastor or associate pastor as the guest speaker. Tell why you invited him to come.

13. Complete a Scripture search, looking for biblical reasons to enter and remain in accountability relationships:
Proverbs 13:10,14,18,20; 15:31-33; 27:6,17; Romans 12:9-16; 15:1-2,14; Galatians 5:25–6:2.

14. Lead a Scripture search to find several well-known biblical accountability relationships. Have groups identify the setting in each instance. Allow for brief discussions of the relationships.
    (a) Peter, James, and John—Matthew 17:1
    (b) Elizabeth and Mary—Luke 1:39-45
    (c) Aquila, Priscilla, and Apollos—Acts 18:24-26
    (d) Paul and Timothy—2 Timothy 2:1-2

15. Close with prayer, asking God to guide learners as they seek to be accountable first to Him and then to significant others in their lives.

### After the Session

1. Read next week's content and complete the learning activities. Follow the suggestions in "Before the Session."

2. Pray for each member of your class by name. Pray especially for anyone who may have been defensive about the concept of accountability. Would it be possible for your class to become more vulnerable, teachable, available, and honest with each other? How?

3. Contact visitors and members who may have missed class recently. Let them know they are missed.

# Break Old Habits

day One

## Winning the Battle Over Greed

I know of nothing that takes longer, is harder work, or requires greater effort than breaking the old habits that hold us in the grip of mediocrity.

Four major enemies must be identified and attacked if we hope for excellence in our Christian lives: *greed, traditionalism, apathetic indifference,* and *joyless selfishness.* And we shall take them in that order. Today let's take a brief yet close look at *greed.*

### GREED UNDER THE SCOPE

Practically speaking, *greed* is an inordinate desire for more, an excessive, unsatisfied hunger to possess. Like an untamed beast, greed grasps, claws, reaches, clutches, and clings—stubbornly refusing to surrender. The word *enough* is not in this beast's vocabulary. Greed is always insatiably craving, longing, wanting, striving for more, more, more.

> **Why do you think a promotion at work, a sign of good performance, is almost always associated with a raise in salary?** _____
>
> **Read Matthew 6:24 and 1 Timothy 6:10. Explain the lurking danger of wanting more and more money?**

_____

### FOUR FACES OF GREED

The first and most common face greed wears is the green mask of money, money, money! *Greed is an excessive motivation to have more money.* Most often, greed appears as a gnawing, ruthless hunger to get more, to earn more, and even to hoard more money. It is a face we see all around us. Most people are woefully discontented with their salary. And by the way, you don't have to be rich to be greedy. I know more

Using the letters of the word *greed,* list five things you are now or have been greedy about:

G _____
R _____
E _____
E _____
D _____

**131**

people who haven't enough money who are greedy than I know who have more than they need.

Second, greed often wears the face of things, material possessions. *Greed is an excessive determination to own more things.* We never quite have enough furniture. Or the right furniture. Have you noticed? We never have the right carpet or just the drapes we'd like to have. And then there's the woodwork like we've always dreamed of having. Or the car we've always wanted to own. Whether it's little trinkets we happen to collect or some big thing like a home or a RV or a boat—it's always something. It's that driving desire to own more things. To say it straight, greed is raw, unchecked materialism.

Third, greed can wear the face of fame. *Greed is also an excessive desire to become more famous, to make a name for oneself.* Some are so determined to be stars, to be in lights, they'd stop at nothing to have people quote them or to be seen in celebrity circles. Thankfully, not all who are famous fall into the greedy category. It's wonderful to meet people who are stars and don't know it.

Fourth, greed can wear the face of control. Such *greed is an excessive need to gain more control*—to gain mastery over something or someone, to always be in charge, to call all the shots, to become the top dog, the king of the hill. The great goal in many people's lives is to manipulate their way to the top of whichever success ladder they choose to climb.

At the risk of sounding terribly simplistic in my analysis, greed can be traced back in Scripture to that day our original parents, Adam and Eve, fell in the garden. When they turned their attention from the living God back to themselves, greed entered and polluted the human bloodstream. It has contaminated human nature ever since. In order for our greed to be controlled, a fight is inevitable. It is a battle for you, and it is a battle for me.

### Circle *agree* or *disagree* after reading these sentences.

agree  disagree  1. I like to be in control.

agree  disagree  2. I like for people to notice me.

agree  disagree  3. I generally buy on credit.

agree  disagree  4. I trade for a new car before my previous car is paid for.

agree  disagree  5. I don't have a regular savings plan.

agree  disagree  6. I have a balance on my credit card.

agree  disagree  7. I will only live in certain neighborhoods.

**If you circled *agree* more than *disagree*, spend this next month monitoring your expenditures. Then ask yourself, what does my review say about my battle with greed?**

Our Lord realized what a hold material things can have on humanity. In no less than seventeen of His thirty-seven parables, Jesus dealt with property and the responsibility for using it wisely. One of those stories seems significant enough for us to examine.

# Greed Exposed and Denounced

What we find in Luke 12:13-34 is one of the clearest and most forthright discourses on greed that you'll find anywhere in all of literature.

Let me summarize the Luke 12 account into four parts. In verses 13-14 there's a dialogue. In verse 15 Jesus gives a brief principle. In verses 16-21 there's a story that Jesus tells about a greedy man who made his living as a successful farmer. Then in verses 22-34 we shall find a series of truths.

## THE DIALOGUE

According to verses 13-14, out of the crowd emerges a man who boldly tells Jesus what to do. Interestingly, he neither asks a question nor makes a request. The man doesn't graciously say "Please." There isn't even a "Sir." He has the audacity to instruct Jesus on what to do.

Knowing how complicated and counterproductive such family squabbles can be, Jesus refrained. But apparently Jesus heard in the tone of the man's voice, or realized from the issue that was raised (a family inheritance), that this was a perfect place to address the bigger issue of greed.

"And someone in the crowd said to Him, 'Teacher, tell my brother to divide the family inheritance with me.' But He said to him, 'Man, who appointed Me a judge or arbiter over you?'" (Luke 12:13-14).

## THE PRINCIPLE

Don't miss the pronouns in verses 14-15. In verse 14, "He said to *him*." But in verse 15, "He said to *them*." Jesus answers the man in verse 14, but then He turns to the crowd and speaks to *them* about a broader subject. In doing so, He declares a warning: "Watch out—be on guard!"

About what? "Be on your guard against every form of greed." Jesus employs the word *form*. Greed has many forms.

The Greeks had a curious word they used when referring to *greed*. The word used in verse 15 means "a thirst for having more." This thing is like a cancer—an insatiable leech that will suck the life right out of you. Enough will never be enough, which explains the reason our Lord adds: "for not even when one has an abundance does his life consist of his possessions." Life does not—*cannot*—revolve around things if one hopes to achieve true excellence. The battle with greed must be won if we hope to soar in the Christian life.

"And He said to them, 'Beware, and be on your guard against every form of greed; for not even when one has an abundance does his life consist of his possessions'" (Luke 12:15).

### What "forms" of greed do you find most tempting?

1. _____

2. _____

3. _____

### THE PARABLE

Read verses 16-21. Before we call down wholesale condemnation upon this farmer, let's be sure we understand that the man is not wrong because he is successful and prosperous. Furthermore, he's not wrong because he is lazy. Neither do we find one word here about the man's being dishonest. He hasn't earned a dishonest living. On the contrary, he's apparently been very diligent and careful as a farmer. There's nothing wrong with a bumper crop—or with any of the things that brought him to prosperity. Then, what is wrong?

I find three glaring, tragic failures about this man.

First: *He didn't really know himself.* It never entered his mind that he might not live for many years to come; he talked to his soul as if he were immortal. He also never stopped to consider that his abundance would never, ever satisfy his soul down deep inside. Remember what he said? "Take your ease, eat, drink, and be merry." Those are words of false satisfaction, of presumption. He was so preoccupied with the temporal that he didn't bother to give eternal thoughts the time of day. Such horizontal thinking is the epitome of a mediocre lifestyle.

Second: *He didn't really care about other people.* His remarks are thoroughly, completely, unashamedly full of himself. He is occupying the throne of his own life. In the English version of my Bible, I count six "I's" and five "my's." Never once do we find "they," "them," "their"—

no, not even once. Why? Because he doesn't care about "they," "them," and "their." He cares only about "I," "me," and "my." Greed personified.

Third: *The man didn't really make room for God.* He lived his entire life in the tight radius of himself, just as if there were no God. Imagine the shock when the death angel said to him, "You fool! Tonight is curtains! It's over, man—it's all over. Then to whom are you going to leave all these things? Who will have the right to these things that you've prepared?"

> **Compare yourself with the farmer in Jesus' parable. Write (T) true or (F) false for each sentence.**
>
> ___ 1. I don't really know myself very well.
> ___ 2. I care mostly about myself.
> ___ 3. I need to make more room for God in my life.

## A SERIES OF TRUTHS

Notice what comes next in verse 22: "He said to His disciples." See the difference? In verse 14 Jesus spoke to the man, and in verse 15 Jesus addressed the crowd. But finally Jesus gets alone with His twelve and talks with His closest friends—the disciples.

Read verses 22-34. Here's what I learn from all these negative commands. *Those who lose the battle with greed are characterized by anxiety and a pursuit of the temporal.*

But I also notice several positive commands in Jesus' speech. These positives lead me to a second major truth: *Those who win the battle over greed realize their value in God's sight and simply trust Him.*

> **Dr. Swindoll tells us what he learned from the commands in verses 22-34—both the negative and the positive. Without using a name, write about an individual who fits the description of either extreme.**
>
> _____
> _____
> _____

When we arrive at Jesus' powerful conclusion (vv. 33-34), a third truth emerges: *Overcoming greed requires deliberate and assertive action.* "Sell! Give! Make!" Those are demanding imperatives.

Finally, a fourth truth comes from Jesus' words in verse 34 "where your treasure is, there your heart will be." *Personal valuables—real valuables—are sealed in our hearts.*

# day Three

# Slaying the Dragon
# of Traditionalism

Let's be careful to identify the right opponent. It isn't *tradition* per se; it's *traditionalism*. I'm not trying to be petty, only accurate. The right kind of traditions give us deep roots—a solid network of reliable truth in a day when everything seems up for grabs. Among such traditions are those strong statements and principles that tie us to the mast of truth when storms of uncertainty create frightening waves of change driven by winds of doubt. Some of those essentials are: believing in the authority of holy Scripture, knowing and loving God, bowing to the Lordship of Jesus Christ, committing ourselves to others, and becoming people of genuine encouragement. Such traditions are valuable absolutes that keep us from feeling awash in a world of relativism and uncertainty.

In case you haven't noticed, we are specifically commanded to cling to the traditions of faith: "stand firm and hold to the traditions which you were taught" (2 Thessalonians 2:15). Even though many—the majority, in fact—will elect to walk a contrary path, "not according to the tradition" which Scripture clearly asserts, we are instructed to stay on target (2 Thessalonians 3:6).

There is a great deal of difference between tradition and traditional-*ism*. By traditionalism, I have in mind mainly an attitude that resists change, adaptation, or alteration. It is holding fast to a custom or behavior that is being blindly and forcefully maintained. It is being suspicious of the new, the up-to-date, the different. It is finding one's security, even identity, in the familiar and therefore opposing whatever threatens that. And if you'll allow me one more, it is substituting a legalistic system for the freedom and freshness of the Spirit—being more concerned about keeping rigid, manmade rules than being flexible, open to creativity and innovation.

By now you've guessed where I stand. Clearly, my position is on the side of openness, allowing room for the untried, the unpredictable, the unexpected—all the while holding fast to the truth. When this philosophy is embraced, eagle eggs are laid, eagles are hatched, and eagles are given room to fly. When traditionalism rules the roost, you can expect nothing but parrots—low-flying creatures that stay on a perch and mimic only what they are told to say. Believe me, there are plenty of people around who feel it is their calling to tell others what to do and what to say. They are self-appointed wing-clippers who frown on new ways and put down high flight.

**_Circle_ the words or phrases you consider traditions. _Underline_ words or phrases you consider traditionalism.**

| | | |
|---|---|---|
| baptism | order of worship | Lord's Supper |
| hymns | fasting | praise choruses |
| choir robes | moderator | prayer walking |
| Doxology | church architecture | |

**day Four**

What image or picture comes to your mind when you hear the word *Pharisee?* Jot down your thoughts here:

# First-Century Traditionalism

**Read the following Scriptures and explain why Jesus was correct in using a bridegroom analogy to speak to the Pharisees: Revelation 19:7-9; 21:1-2,9.**

In Jesus' day the dragon of traditionalism was synonymous with Pharisaism. The Pharisees embraced it, promoted it, and modeled it. A classic case in point is found in Luke 5:27-39.

A fellow named Matthew (called Levi by Dr. Luke) was invited to leave his profession as a tax-gatherer and become a follower of Jesus. He did. In fact, he threw a party at his place in honor of the Master. Naturally, the place was packed with guys Levi had run around with for years—fellow tax men and other cronies, none of them religious but all of them his friends and colleagues.

There was a lot of telling and sharing and listening to stories. They were having a whale of a good time together, just plain fun—except, of course, for the Pharisees. I can just imagine their standing outside, looking in the window, staring and not smiling. The tax-gatherers and other friends, along with Jesus and His disciples, were reclining at the table together. But when the religious hotshots heard the noise, verse 30 tells us, they began taking verbal shots at Jesus and His men.

You see, the main problem was that the disciples of Jesus were mixing with and enjoying themselves among the sinner types. The Pharisees believed (and taught!) that they should remain separate from these types. Did you notice that Luke refers to "tax-gatherers and other people" (v. 29), but when he quotes the Pharisees the phrase changes to "tax-gatherers and *sinners*" (v. 30)?

The disciples are speechless. They don't know what to say. Completely unintimidated by the presence of Pharisees, Jesus gave them a straight answer: "It is not those who are well who need a physician, but those who are sick" (v. 31). If that isn't enough to slam them to the mat, read on: "I have not come to call righteous men but sinners to repentance" (v. 32). Stab . . . twist.

Well, if you think the Pharisees left Him alone after that, you don't understand the nature of the dragon traditionalism. All that meant to them was that the coin had been flipped and it was time to kick off. The game was on, and the Pharisees answer Jesus with "The disciples of John often fast and offer prayers; the disciples of the Pharisees also do the same; but Yours eat and drink" (v. 33).

That is supposed to be a sarcastic put-down. "You may have time for this jesting, but not us! This is serious business. We're into fasting. You and Your people are in there eating and drinking with those nasty sinners and having fun. Don't You know that life is much too serious for all this?"

Look at Jesus' answer in verse 34: "And Jesus said to them, 'You cannot make the attendants of the bridegroom fast while the bridegroom is with them, can you?'" What a superb rebuttal! Back then, as long as the bridegroom was around, it was nonstop eating and drinking, laughing and having fun—constant rejoicing. But when the bridegroom left, it got sad because everyone had to go back to work. Thus Jesus added, "But the days will come; and when the bridegroom is taken away from them, then they will fast in those days" (v. 35).

The Pharisees were strangely silent. They stared, struggling to grasp His meaning. Apparently, they were unable to piece it together so Jesus tells them a brief story. Notice His approach in verse 36. He does it in a simple, disarming way. He does it with comments having to do with old and new garments, with old and new wine.

Anyone who has had new clothing shrink would understand. Jesus is using clothing as His subject, but He has something deeper in mind (would you believe, traditionalism?). You see, these Pharisees were committed to the old. They majored in *ancient* history, and they swore by the Law. They were set in concrete into the precepts and statutes of the Law. They could quote those words exactly as they appeared on the ancient scroll of the Torah. To make matters worse, they added over six hundred additional rules (really!) so everybody would understand how *they* interpreted the way everyone should live. And they were rigid about it! You see, they are the "old garment." Jesus' point: You can't match something new with something old. It will tear away.

Jesus then drives His point home by speaking of wine in verse 37. Just as He wasn't talking about literal old and new fabrics, neither is He talking about literal wine and wineskins. This is a parable, remember—a story that uses the literal and familiar to teach the spiritual and unfamiliar. Jesus' audience understood that these words were missiles carrying a massive payload. Jesus presses His point home in verse 38. Hmmmm. All of a sudden, the picture is coming into clear focus, which makes the Pharisees terribly nervous. You know why? Because Jesus says, in effect, "You like the old." As Jesus said in verse 39, "And no one, after drinking old wine wishes for new; for he says, 'The old is good enough.'"

The old Judaic-traditionalism skin could not contain the new wine of the revolutionary gospel Christ was offering. It split the skin. There the Pharisees stood, representing all those manmade regulations, observing this revolutionary, risky message about liberty, grace, freedom, forgiveness, deliverance from the Law, compassion, and hope. But their wineskin couldn't contain it. They were so entrenched and inflexible, the new wine dripped through. Finally, it burst the bag completely. The old simply could not contain the new.

"No one tears a piece from a new garment and puts it on an old garment; otherwise he will both tear the new, and the piece from the new will not match the old" (Luke 5:36).

"And no one puts new wine into old wineskins; otherwise the new wine will burst the skins, and it will be spilled out, and the skins will be ruined" (Luke 5:37).

"But new wine must be put into fresh wineskins" (Luke 5:38).

**As seen from other New Testament passages, what to the Pharisees was risky and new about Jesus' teachings as they related to the topics on the top of page 140?**

Grace (Ephesians 2:8-10) _____

Freedom (John 8:31-36; Galatians 5:1) _____

_____

Forgiveness (Matthew 6:14-15; 1 John 1:8-10) _____

_____

The Law (Galatians 2:15-16,21) _____

Oh, but how the Pharisees loved their own traditions! They preferred them to the Truth of God, believe it or not. Matthew's account includes a rebuke from Jesus to the Pharisees about how they were holding their traditions so tightly that they were resisting God's revelation. His rebuke? "You invalidated the word of God for the sake of your traditions" (Matthew 15:6).

Let's face it—truth that sets people free is the greatest threat to traditionalism.

day *Five*

# Modern Day Traditionalism

A couple of very significant things seem to jump out at me when I think about Jesus' parable. First: *God is a God of freshness and change.*

But wait, let me make something very clear: God Himself isn't changing, nor is His Son. He "is the same yesterday and today, yes and forever" (Hebrews 13:8). Isn't that a great thought? God is no different this year than He was last year or a decade ago. Nor will He change one hundred years from now. But even though He is the same, His working is different. It stays fresh. His ways and methods are forever fresh, unpredictably new.

If you like things to stay the same, you're going to be terribly uncomfortable in heaven. Everything is going to be new. God is a God of freshness and change. He flexes His methods. He alters His way so much, it's as if you've never seen it before. You can't imagine what it may be like next time.

How does this personally apply? Ephesians 5:1 says, "Therefore be imitators of God, as beloved children." God says we are to be "imitators" of Him, which really means we are to "mimic" Him. Since God is a God of freshness and change, so we should be. If we are to fulfill this command "to be mimics of God, as His beloved children," then I suggest that we stay fresh—that we remain open, innovative, willing to change.

It's been my observation that every generation tends to be more strict and rigid than the last. We tend to tighten the lid tighter on traditionalism. Even though our God of freshness and change has given us all those vats of new wine to use, we'll not let go of the old; we'll find ways to conserve it, to protect it, to maintain it, to save it. But those who resist mediocrity in the Christian life are models of innovation.

Now for the second significant fact I see from Luke 5: *New wineskins are essential, not optional.* Every age knows the temptation to try to restrict God's dealings. The majority of people in this world are maintainers. Once we get things set, we don't like them changed.

We must guard against wrapping the Christianity of the 21st-century in the garb of the 1960s or 1970s or 1980s! If we're not careful, we'll become so committed to "the way we were" we'll dull the cutting edge of relevance and leave this generation in the dust. I repeat: NEW WINESKINS ARE ESSENTIAL. It's us. We're the skin. If we hope to soar for Christ in the 21st century, we *must* come to terms with rigidity. The dragon of traditionalism *must* be slain!

What about your wineskin? Is your wineskin still flexible? Are you ready to move? Are you open to change in your whole career? Are you willing to risk? Are you flexible enough to innovate? Are you willing to tolerate the sheer possibility of making a massive change in your direction for life? It may mean moving across the street. It may mean moving across the States. It may mean moving across the seas. It may not involve a move at all, only a willingness. People who make a difference have supple wineskins. They can be stretched, pulled, pushed, and changed.

Out with the dragon of traditionalism! This is a new year, a new generation, a new era.

**Has the gospel set you free or bottled you up? Write a prayer asking God to prepare you to stay fresh—open, innovative, and willing to change.**

---

Have you ever had someone mimic you?
❏ Yes    ❏ No

How would it make you feel for someone to mimic you—angry or flattered? _____

How does God feel when we mimic Him?
_____

## Before the Session

1. On posterboard or tear sheets prepare a chart. Title the left hand side "Overcoming Greed" and the right hand side "Action Plan." Down the left hand side print these four statements in descending order: (1.) Pursue the eternal; (2.) Realize your value in God's sight; (3.) Trust God as provider; (4.) Seal valuables in your heart.

2. Optional: Invite a church member to your class who has an inspiring story of overcoming greed or of generosity in supporting God's work. Allow no more than 10 minutes for the testimony.

## During the Session

1. Welcome participants and open with prayer requests and prayer.

2. Review last week's lesson. Introduce today's study with Dr. Swindoll's warning that old habits hold us in the grip of mediocrity. Ask someone to name the two habits we are seeking to break in today's lesson (greed, traditionalism).

3. Select four volunteers to list the four faces of greed and give an example of each. Then ask, *Why did Jesus have so much to say about the responsible use of money and property?* Assign someone to read aloud Matthew 6:24 and 1 Timothy 6:10,17-19 as part of the discussion.

4. Enlist someone to read the verses from Luke 12 in four parts: verses 13-14; verse 15; verses 16-21; verses 22-34. After each part, review the Bible truths from Dr. Swindoll's material in Day 2.

5. Reveal the chart posted on a focal wall. Form four groups. Assign each group one of the four principles for overcoming greed. (See Day 2 under "A Series of Truths.") Ask each group to develop an action plan to establish the principle in our lives.

6. Optional: Introduce the person enlisted in advance to give his/her testimony concerning overcoming greed or giving generously. Another suggestion would be to have volunteers to share their responses to the last learning activity of Day 2.

7. Announce that the group is now turning its attention to traditionalism, the second habit that needs to be broken in order to escape

---

Don't allow this session to become a "gripe" session for either side of the tradition vs traditionalism issue. Focus on Bible truths and Dr. Swindoll's stimulating content.

NOTES

mediocrity. Read Dr. Swindoll's definition of traditionalism in the third paragraph of Day 3.

8. Select someone to read 2 Thessalonians 2:15; 3:6. Ask a volunteer to explain the difference between *tradition* and *traditionalism*. As a group, complete the first learning activity in Day 3. Allow some room for disagreement.

9. Invite someone to review Dr. Swindoll's analogy from Day 3 of an eagle and a parrot (one represents tradition; the other traditionalism). Ask, *Which are you in your Christian life?*

10. From the material in Day 4 point out that traditionalism is not a new problem. Read aloud around the circle Luke 5:27-39. Interrupt the reading as needed to review Dr. Swindoll's commentary on these verses.

11. Invite members to share their responses to the learning activity in Day 4 that asked them to identify Jesus' "risky teachings." Quiz members to insure that they understand the differences between Jesus' teachings and the teachings of the Pharisees and Sadducees.

12. Read 2 Corinthians 5:17 and Hebrews 13:8. Ask someone to state the paradox found in these verses. Discuss how Christians should seek to walk in the tension between an unchanging gospel and innovative ways of sharing it with new generations.

13. Ask members to bow their heads and close their eyes. Ask these questions, allowing a pause between them for members to answer them silently:

    (1.) *How would your church friends describe you: traditional or traditionalistic?*

    (2.) *Concerning traditionalism, are you part of the problem in our church or part of the solution?*

14. Close with a spoken prayer.

## After the Session

1. Read next week's content and complete the learning activities. Follow the suggestions in "Before the Session."

2. Pray for each member of your class by name. Pray especially for anyone who may have been defensive about the concept of traditionalism. Could your class lead the way in supporting your leaders as they try to lead your church in new and innovative ways?

3. Contact visitors and members who may have missed class recently. Let them know they are missed.

# Fight Fiercely

day One

## Removing the Blahs from Today

Monotony and mediocrity mesh like teeth in gears. One spawns the other, leaving us yawning, bored, and adrift. In referring to monotony, I do not have in mind a lack of activity as much as a lack of purpose. We can be busy yet bored, involved yet indifferent. Life becomes tediously repetitious, dull, humdrum, pedestrian. In a word, *blah.*

Who would ever expect such a thing to be an enemy? Seems too mild, too passive to even mention. Not so! It is one of the deadliest darts in the Devil's quiver. Once it strikes, the poison spreads rapidly, leaving us listless, careless, and disillusioned. Show me an individual who once soared, whose life was characterized by enthusiasm and excellence, but who no longer reaches those heights, and I'll show you a person who has probably become a victim of the *blahs*—the *blahs* of monotony and indifference.

**Measure your "blah" index for today. 1 = low "blah" index and 5 = high "blah" index.**

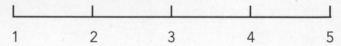

| 1 | 2 | 3 | 4 | 5 |

Surely, if this sneaky opponent of excellence is that powerful, there ought to be some insights and techniques that help us fight it out in the trenches. Indeed there are! Believe it or not, they find their source in a prayer written by Moses many centuries ago.

### A PRAYER WITH A PUNCH

Psalm 90 is the only psalm specifically attributed to Moses. He may have written others, but we know for sure he wrote this one. Remember Moses? Most think of him as a man of action, an aggressive leader, point man in the exodus, outspoken giver of the Law. But it is easy to overlook the repetitious, monotonous routine he endured. Between ages forty and eighty, Moses led his father-in-law's flock of sheep in the desert. Following the exodus, he led the Hebrews another forty years as they wandered across and around the wilderness. I'd say he knew about the *blahs*. Same terrain, same scenes, same route, same ornery people, same negative outlook, same complaints, same miserable weather, same *everything!* The prayer he wrote could have been his means of maintaining sanity!

**Now return to the "blah" index. Where would you put a mark for Moses during the majority of his ministry?**

## BREAKING THE SPELL

Frequently, our problem with boredom begins when we fall under monotony's "spell." In this quasi-hypnotic state, we get sucked into a bland "who cares?" mentality. Mediocrity and passive cynicism await those who let themselves get trapped. How are we to cope? We must direct our attention to (a) the right object that we might gain and (b) the right perspective. Moses addresses his Lord specifically (vv. 1,2,13,17) and spells out His personal involvement in everyday affairs. Read Psalm 90:1-2 in the margin.

As this ancient shepherd-leader did, we too must begin by crying out to our God: "Lord!" What a relief to be able to call on Him! In doing so, it helps to rehearse before Him our real place of residence. It isn't here on this measly piece of real estate called Earth. It is with Him. Did you get that? "Lord—*You* are my home . . . my habitation . . . my hiding place." Moses goes even further, moving back through God's creative work to eternity itself. If we take our minds as far back as possible, we arrive at the vanishing point of the past—infinity. Moses is saying: "God, even at the vanishing point of the past and the future—the most distant place we can imagine—You are there!"

"Lord, Thou hast been our dwelling place in all generations. Before the mountains were born, or Thou didst give birth to the earth and the world, even from everlasting to everlasting, Thou art God" (Psalm 90:1-2).

We can't fathom such a journey. We can only imagine it. But when we go as far back as possible in our minds (the vanishing point of the past) and step off, there is God. And when we project ourselves to the vanishing point of the future, the misty infinity of tomorrow, again there is our God.

What he is saying is this: As I go from the vanishing point of yesterday to the vanishing point of tomorrow and find that God is present, then there is not a place in the entire scope of my everyday existence where God is not there. And to make it even more personal, there is purpose, there is meaning in the presence of God. Even in the things that we may consider to be pointless, insignificant, trivial.

**How do you feel about always being in the presence of God? Circle one or more of the words below.**

| | | | |
|---|---|---|---|
| uncomfortable | anxious | shy | hopeful |
| intimidated | scared | courageous | peaceful |
| purposeful | comfortable | confident | thrilled |

Don't miss the right perspective: "From everlasting to everlasting, Thou art *God.*" From my yesterday to my tomorrow—God. From the little involvements to the big ones—God. From the beginning of school to the end of school—God. From the assignments that will never really make the headlines all the way to those things that gain international attention—God. From my children's earliest years to our last year together—God! You are in it, Lord. You're there! Yes, even when everything goes wrong.

Try this. The very next time you feel those clammy, cold fingers of the *blahs* reaching around you, remember, "From yesterday until tomorrow, You, O Lord, are there, You care!" It will help you mount up with wings as an eagle. I know. I have put it to the test numerous times.

**What is God doing as He is there around you (Psalm 90:1)?** _____

**What is the purpose of a dwelling place?** _____
_____

# Probing the Soul

So much for breaking the spell. Probing the soul takes up where that leaves off. As I probe my soul during times of such wrestlings, almost without exception, I find three thoughts washing around in my head.

**As you read, fill in the blanks to complete Dr. Swindoll's three thoughts about Psalm 90:3-5:**

Life is so _____.

My _____ are so obvious.

My days are so _____.

First, I think: *Life is so short.* We really don't have many years. And to spend them doing dumb stuff seems like such a waste. Read Psalm 90:3-5.

Talk about vivid word pictures! Life moves so rapidly it is as if we have been swept through time like a *flood.* Quickly passing as a three-hour *watch* in the night, like *yesterday!* And then we fall asleep and die. Read verses 5-6. Another reminder of the brevity of life: "Toward evening it fades, and withers away" like *grass.*

Those thoughts have a way of haunting a person who really wants his life to amount to more than just a tiny period printed on the page of time, don't they? We want to offer at least a sentence. But what I see growing out of these lines in Moses' prayer is that it is God who controls our marks in this world. He sets the limit. In fact, He's the One who says, "Return, O children of men." And without hesitation, they return. What seems all-important can change almost overnight. When the Controller says, "Return," it's amazing how quickly that return can occur.

Look again at Moses' prayer. He brings up a second thought that plagues me when the *blahs* come: *My sins are so obvious.* Do you ever feel like that in the midst of this routine called life and time? Sure you do. Moses did, too. Read verses 7-9.

Remember the secret sin that haunted Moses—the murder of that Egyptian? I wonder how many rocks he walked around in the desert only to hear that same skeleton rattle. I cannot imagine how many days he must have finished with "a sigh." Couldn't hide it, couldn't dodge it, couldn't deny it. "My sins are so obvious, Lord. How can I put it all together? I am weary of feeling the stinging reminder of Your wrath!" Immediately on the heels of those feelings, Moses writes verse 10. These are the words of a man who feels cornered by an attack of the *blahs.*

Yes, life is short. Yes, our sins are obvious; no one can deny that. And if those thoughts aren't hard enough to handle, there's a third feeling: *My days are so empty.* Read Moses' grand desire in verse 12.

Look at the word *teach*—"teach us." The word means "cause to know." And the word *number* means "to reckon" or "assign" or "appoint" some-

"Thou dost turn man back into dust, and dost say, 'Return, O children of men.' For a thousand years in Thy sight are like yesterday when it passes by, or as a watch in the night. Thou hast swept them away like a flood, they fall asleep" (Psalm 90:3-5).

"In the morning they are like grass which sprouts anew. In the morning it flourishes, and sprouts anew; towards evening it fades, and withers away" (Psalm 90:5-6).

"For we have been consumed by Thine anger, and by Thy wrath we have been dismayed. Thou hast placed our iniquities before Thee, our secret sins in the light of Thy presence. For all our days have declined in Thy fury; we have finished our years like a sigh" (Psalm 90:7-9).

"As for the days of our life, they contain seventy years, or if due to strength, eighty years, yet their pride is but labor and sorrow; for soon it is gone and we fly away" (Psalm 90:10).

"So teach us to number our days, that we may present to Thee a heart of wisdom" (Psalm 90:12).

thing. One lexicon suggests the phrase "that we may present to Thee" could be rendered "that we may gain." All these observations lead me to this paraphrase of verse 12: "So cause us to know how to assign significance to our days so that we may gain the ability to see life as You see it." That is what we need to do for us to keep on soaring in the Christian life, we need to learn how to make our days *significant* days.

**How do you try to make each day significant? Check one or more.**

❑ 1. Significant? Dr. Swindoll doesn't know my boring routine.
❑ 2. I guess some people might find my job repetitious, but I enjoy the people I work with.
❑ 3. I know I do a good job, and that is very satisfying.
❑ 4. The Christian life is an adventure. You never know what God is up to next!

day Three

# Bringing the Song

Is there a particular Christian song that you find yourself singing when you break through the blahs?

What is the title of your song? _____
_____

After breaking the spell and probing the soul, the psalmist introduces us to a very special song, "Do return, O Lord; how long will it be? And be sorry for Thy servants" (v. 13). The idea is for God to have pity upon them. The song continues: "O satisfy us in the morning with Thy lovingkindness, that we may sing for joy and be glad all our days" (v. 14). It sounds to me as if Moses has broken through the *blahs*. I don't know about you, but with me it often happens in the morning. The night before may have seemed dark and dreary. Those night hours are often the backwash of boredom. By morning, however—usually early, when there's sort of a fresh breath of air, the smog is gone, and the day is cool —it is amazing how God brings something fresh. Psalm 30:5 also describes this feeling of renewal: "For His anger is but for a moment, His favor is for a lifetime; weeping may last for the night, but a shout of joy comes in the morning."

After the satisfaction that comes from fresh joy in the morning, there is restoration: "Make us glad according to the days Thou hast afflicted us, and the years we have seen evil" (v. 15). The phrase "according to the days Thou hast afflicted us" seemed troubling to me when I first read it. Then I noticed that the marginal reference in my *New American Standard Bible* suggests "Make us glad *as many days* as Thou hast afflicted us." Now I understand. "Lord, when You bring satisfaction to what seemed to me to be a monotonous life, that satisfaction is in proportion to the days that once seemed meaningless." *The Living Bible* says, "Give us gladness in proportion to our former misery." God has a way of balancing out the good with the bad.

**Think of an example from your own life of God's balancing out the good with the bad.** _____

_____

Finally, after all that, there is motivation—"Let Thy work appear to Thy servants, and Thy majesty to their children" (v. 16)—and confirmation—"And let the favor of the Lord our God be upon us; and do confirm for us the work of our hands; yes, confirm the work of our hands" (v. 17).

*Confirm* means "to give meaning, to make permanent." It is this idea: "Cause me to see it as significant." Instead of my thinking of these days as just about as futile as emptying wastebaskets, help me to see the significance of them in light of Your plan. When God confirms the work of our hands, He helps us see the value of the routine, the importance of what we once considered mundane, humdrum—the same ol' thing.

In the monotonous assignments of daily living, God can take something that seems routine and dull and use it as a platform on which to do His significant work. Remember this: Those who achieve excellence are faithful in the tedious, monotonous details of life. It is there amidst the *blahs* of boredom that we rise above the level of mediocrity and soar.

**Can you name some biblical characters who were going about their daily chores when God intervened and changed their lives forever? List as many as you can.**

_____   _____

_____   _____

_____   _____

# Becoming a Model of Joyful Generosity

I cannot grasp how anyone can justify a continual long face. Surely, God never intended such! And it isn't just a matter of personality. Or simply a matter of temperament. It's mostly a matter of the heart and often a matter of habit. We need to be ever alert to joylessness—an enemy that will break and enter, robbing us of one of life's most prized possessions.

> "The Bible frequently connects a laughing heart with a giving hand."
> – Charles Swindoll

**Where are you most of the time on the giver scale?**

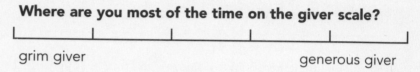

grim giver                                   generous giver

Joylessness is never a more evident enemy than when the subject of giving surfaces. But if I read God's Book correctly, He takes no delight in a grim giver, but rather in a cheerful one. He loves it when hilarity and generosity meet at the offering plate! When they do, I have this sneaking suspicion that He smiles broadly. To the surprise of many, the Bible frequently connects a laughing heart with a giving hand. So I think it might be best to approach this subject of joy from the viewpoint of being generous as well.

Two letters in the New Testament were written to the church at Corinth. Both were from the same man, Paul, who spent a little over a year and a half getting that particular church established. The Corinthian church was loaded with potential. It had numerous spiritual gifts and fine teachers. It had money and influence. But it also had some people who reverted to carnality. These people had made great promises to God regarding their commitment, but only a few months later they'd grown cold and backed off. They needed to be reminded of what they had promised God. That is part of the reason Paul wrote them—actually, the major reason he wrote them the second letter.

You see, many miles removed from Corinth was another church, much older, and struggling financially. I'm referring to the mother church in Jerusalem. That church, though older, was now economically strapped. Their need for assistance was acute. So Paul was involved in raising funds for the Jerusalem church, a project which brought him to the region of Macedonia, just north of Corinth.

Even though the Macedonian Christians were also in an economically depressed area, Paul appealed to them, urging them to respond to the needs in Jerusalem. The Macedonians gave generously—abundantly, in fact. A year earlier the Corinthians also had promised to give to this need. When word reached Paul that the Corinthians had long since set aside this project and had failed in their efforts to raise the funds they promised to give, he decided to write them to remind them of their previous commitment.

Read 2 Corinthians 9:1-3. In these verses Paul is saying that if he were to bring some Macedonian Christians with him to Corinth and have them pick up the measly Corinthian offering to take back to Jerusalem, he would be red-faced. Why? Because it was the Corinthian example (Paul had mentioned them to those in Macedonia) that prompted the Macedonians to give over and above their ability. So he writes to spur them on. Drawing on an age-old agricultural analogy, he begins: "Now this I say, he who sows sparingly shall also reap sparingly; and he who sows bountifully shall also reap bountifully" (v. 6). Then he goes further: "Let each one do just as he has purposed in his heart; not grudgingly or under compulsion" (v. 7). The word *grudgingly* means "reluctantly," the idea of holding onto something because you don't want to part with it.

> "When the heart is full of cheer, it is amazing how it causes the pockets to turn inside out."
> – Charles Swindoll

In this 2 Corinthians passage, we are also instructed not to give under compulsion. That means "feeling forced because of what someone may say or think." You see, compulsion results in even greater reluctance. When we are compelled to do something, we are all the more reluctant to give it up.

I've built to the climax that appears at the end of verse 7: "for God loves a cheerful giver." In the ancient days when the Greek text was written, interesting things occurred in the formation of words in a phrase or sentence. When words were placed out of order at the beginning of a sentence, it was usually for the purpose of emphasis. Guess what appears first in this last sentence: *cheerful*, not *giver*. Not even *God*. No, the word *cheerful* is the first major word to appear in the text: "For the cheerful one, who is a giver, God prizes."

Hover for a moment over the key word *cheerful*. In Greek it is the term *hilaros*, from which we get our word *hilarious*. It is such an unusual word it appears nowhere else in all the New Testament. Several times it surfaces in the Old Testament Greek version of the Bible (the Septuagint), but never any other place in all the New Testament. Literally, the sentence reads, "For the hilarious giver God prizes." Do you know why He prizes the hilarious giver? Because the hilarious giver gives so generously. He has no special possession or gift or skill or amount of money that he grips tightly. No, when the heart is full of cheer, it is amazing how it causes the pockets to turn inside out. Unlike the mediocre majority, those Christians who soar are full of joy that expresses itself in greathearted generosity.

**What attitudes would cause a person not to be a cheerful giver? Be prepared to refute these excuses and add some of your own during the group session.**

    a. I made this money. It's all mine.

    b. But I need _____ (fill in the blank).

    c. No one helped me when I was down.

    d. I'll help when I get my finances straightened out.

## day Five

# Joyful Generosity Can Be Ours Today

> "Bless the Lord, O my soul; and all that is within me, bless His holy name. Bless the Lord, O my soul, and forget none of His benefits; who pardons all your iniquities; who heals all your diseases; who redeems your life from the pit; who crowns you with lovingkindness and compassion; who satisfies your years with good things, so that your youth is renewed like the eagle. The Lord performs righteous deeds, and judgments for all who are oppressed"
> (Psalm 103:1-6).

Let's think about how we can bring some much-needed joy back into our lives today. I have four suggestions in mind.

1. *Reflect on God's gifts to you.* In case you need a little help, read through Psalm 103:1-6. The psalmist lists several benefits to prod our thinking. As we reflect on God's gifts to us, it's helpful to be specific. Do you have eyesight? It's a gift. Do you have a good mind? It's a gift. How about dexterity in your fingers? Or special skills that allow you to work in your occupation? Do you have leadership abilities that cause others to follow? A good education? Do you have the ability to sell? These are all gifts. Has He given you a family? Has He given you sufficient clothes? How about a nice, warm, soft bed at night or a comfortable place to live in the hot summer? Why, some even have more than one home! These are all gifts from God's hand. Reflect on His numerous gifts to you. It will increase your joy. And a smile will soon replace that frown.

2. *Remind yourself of God's promises regarding generosity.* God promises if you sow bountifully, you will reap bountifully. Give abundantly! Even extravagant giving is honored by God. I've never known anyone who went bad because he or she was *too* generous. Remind yourself of God's promises regarding generosity and start releasing!

3. *Examine your heart* (this is going to be the tough one). I don't want you to examine your tax records from last year. That will merely speak to your mind. I want you to talk to your heart. I don't want you to examine your neighbor or some other person, because you will be better than your neighbor or whichever individual you choose. Don't even compare yourself with the way you used to give, because you probably are doing better than you used to do. I challenge you to *examine your heart.* Here are some questions for you to ask yourself:

• Do I really believe there is a need?

• Am I responding out of pressure or because I really care?

• Is my gift an appropriate expression of my income or is it more of a last-minute, unplanned get-it-over-with act?

• Have I prayed or is this impulsive giving?

• Is joy prompting me? Am I genuinely thrilled about what God is doing in my life as well as through my giving?

• Does generosity characterize my life?

4. *Glorify God by being extremely generous.* I think a unique way to look at it is to scare yourself a little. Remember when you didn't have much and you gave more than you should have given, at least for logic's sake? You scared yourself a little, didn't you? Wasn't that fun? Wasn't that absolutely delightful? And the good news is you made it. You didn't starve. Chances are good you are still rather well fed and sufficiently clothed. But are you joyful? Honestly now, has the enemy, Joyless Living, taken charge of you? If so, I can guarantee that you have become less generous. How about cultivating extreme generosity?

Do you know the endless source of joy, Jesus Christ? All that He is and all that He provides is enough to make me laugh out loud!

**Using the space in the margin, change these distorted teachings into Dr. Swindoll's truths for today.**

1. God's never given me much.
2. God never promised me a rose garden.
3. I believe God helps those who help themselves.
4. This is a bad time to be throwing around money. Don't you keep up with the stock market?

Be prepared to recall Dr. Swindoll's four suggestions at the end of today's study.

**Truths for Today:**

1. _____

2. _____

3. _____

4. _____

## Before the Session

1. On posterboard or tear sheets prepare a chart. Title the left hand side "Boring" and the right hand side "Interesting." Mount the chart on a focal wall.
2. Make a poster listing the four steps to regaining joy that Dr. Swindoll lists in Day 5. Mount the poster on a focal wall.

## During the Session

1. As members enter the room, ask them to write something they find boring in the left column and something they find interesting in the right column of the chart on the wall. When most have arrived, welcome participants and open with prayer requests and prayer.
2. Review last week's lesson. Ask, *What were the two habits that we sought to break?* (greed, traditionalism) Ask someone to name the two habits we are seeking to break in today's lesson. (apathetic indifference and joyless selfishness)
3. Call attention to the chart. If the same words have been written in both columns, state the obvious: *What bores me may excite you. A lot depends on our personalities.* Ask, *What types of people do you think are more easily the targets of monotony or apathy?* (passive, unemotional, silent, and so forth) Ask, *What types of jobs might lend themselves to monotony?* (repetitious, routine)
4. Instruct the class to open their Bibles to Psalm 90. Ask members to read aloud around the circle Psalm 90:1-12. Invite volunteers to share what they learned about Moses' life from this Psalm and from Dr. Swindoll's commentary. List responses on a writing surface.
5. Select volunteers to compare times in their lives to times in Moses' life (ups and downs; miraculous moments, times of testing, and so forth)
6. Form groups of 2 to 3 members. Give each group the same assignment: Read Psalm 90: 12. How do you seek to make your days significant? (See Day 2.) At the end of 3-5 minutes of sharing, give individuals the opportunity to report what they said. However, no one should be asked to share who does not volunteer.

Don't mistake activity for purpose. Many of your class members may be very busy yet very adrift spiritually. Seek to identify and meet their needs.

NOTES

7. Summarize the importance of having a sense of God's purpose for your life and daily seeking His plan and His equipping in order to fulfill that purpose. Conversely, discuss the tragedy of any life, especially a Christian life, characterized by routine sameness with no spiritual goals to achieve or no mountaintop experiences with God to look forward to. Have someone read Jeremiah 29:11 and Lamentations 3:22-23.

8. Select a volunteer to read Psalm 90:13-17. Brainstorm characteristics of a joyful giver. Write responses on a writing surface.

9. Invite someone to explain the difference between a joyful giver and one who grips tightly. Ask, *Do you think there is a correlation between what a person earns and the amount he or she gives?* (no) *Why or why not?* (discuss)

10. Call attention to the list of excuses in the learning activity at the end of Day 4. Ask if anyone listed other attitudes that would cause a person not to be a cheerful giver. Then ask the group to refute each of the excuses.

11. Say, *In Day 5 Dr. Swindoll gave us five actions that will bring joy back into our lives if we have been grim givers. However, the activity at the end of Day 5 distorts these principles.* Select volunteers to read a distorted principle from their workbooks on page 153 and then the correct principle from the poster.

12. Ask the class to turn to Psalm 103:1-6 and read aloud in unison this beautiful psalm of praise. Optional: Use the printed Scripture on page 152 to avoid differences in translations while reading in unison.

13. Close with a spoken prayer, thanking God for the gift of Jesus Christ, the true joy-giver.

## After the Session

1. Read next week's content and complete the learning activities. Follow the suggestions in "Before the Session."

2. Pray for each member of your class by name. Pray especially for anyone who may be feeling a lack of direction in his or her spiritual life. Others may be wrestling with the issue of joyful giving. Make yourself available after class for personal ministry.

3. Contact visitors and members who may have missed class recently. Let them know they are missed.

# Stand Courageously

## Standing Alone When Outnumbered

One of the great American myths is that we are all a bunch of rugged individualists. We would like to think that, but it simply is not true. We'd much rather blend into the woodwork. One of our greatest fears is being ostracized, rejected by "the group." Ridicule is a pain too great for most to bear. In the final analysis, whoever decides to soar will be forced to face and come to terms with the great temptation to conform.

Let's look at six observations from Romans 12:1-2.

1. *This truth is mainly for the Christian.* "I urge you, *brethren. . . .*" If I haven't made this clear before, I need to say it straight now. Apart from a personal and vital faith in Jesus Christ, it is impossible to wage a winning effort against the system called "the world." Trying to soar on one's own, overcoming the powerful magnet of the majority without help from above, would be a frustrating and counterproductive effort. Only God can give us such transforming power through our faith in His Son.

2. *There is an urgency in this message—intense urgency, in fact.* Paul doesn't say, "Oh, by the way, it might be nice if. . . ." No, he says, "I *urge* you." The writer is pressing his pen hard; he feels passionate about this. And so must we. No one ever eased effortlessly out of conformity.

3. *This urgency is related to a sacrifice.* The point being, the process of commitment is a "holy sacrifice." We never sacrifice something easily. The whole idea of sacrifice is yielding something that is important to us—releasing, giving over, letting go, surrendering. The urgency will call for sacrifice. Notice that the sacrifice is not only "holy," it is a "living" sacrifice. One of the major problems of a living sacrifice is that it keeps crawling off the altar!

"I urge you therefore, brethren, by the mercies of God, to present your bodies a living and holy sacrifice, acceptable to God, which is your spiritual service of worship. And do not be conformed to this world, but be transformed by the renewing of your mind, that you may prove what the will of God is, that which is good and acceptable and perfect"
(Romans 12:1-2).

**What is meant by a living sacrifice "crawling off the altar"? Check one or more, or write your own.**
- ❏ 1. The sacrifice is an animal.
- ❏ 2. The person gives the sacrifice but is free to take it back at any time.
- ❏ 3. The person is not really sincere about giving it.
- ❏ 4. The living person's commitment vacillates back and forth.

**What would you find difficult to let go?** _____

4. *This sacrifice touches two realms: the inner person and the outer person.* The *inner person* is addressed in the word *present*—"I urge you . . . to present your bodies." This is a decision we make deep down inside ourselves. Next is the *outer person,* "your bodies"—that part of you that touches the system around you. "I urge you by the mercies of God," says Paul, "that you Christians make a deep-down, gut-level decision to present your bodies."

5. *The sacrifice is essentially a spiritual one.* As far as God is concerned, a consistent godly life is well pleasing, acceptable to Him. As far as you are concerned, it is an act of worship. It is a "spiritual service of worship."

I need to be very candid here. If you are a "Sunday Christian," you will not stand alone when outnumbered. Anybody can soar—anyone can walk in victory while sitting in church. But the kind of "service of worship" Romans 12:1-2 is talking about affects your Monday, your Thursday, your Saturday lifestyle—your entire week, in fact, all fifty-two of them every year.

6. *This sacrifice leads to a practical and radical decision.* Look again at the second verse: "Do not be conformed to this world (that is the practical decision), but be transformed by the renewing of your mind (that is the radical decision)."

Let me clarify those thoughts. First, what does it mean to be *conformed?* The word means "to assume an outward expression that does not come from within." When I conform to something, I masquerade; I wrap myself in a mask that isn't true to what I am on the inside.

Second, what does it mean to be *transformed?* The biblical term means "an outward expression that comes from within." Not only is it different, but it is the antithesis of *conform.* The Greek word underlying the term *transformed* here is the verb *metamorphoo,* from which come the English words *metamorphose* and *metamorphosis.* To be "transformed" is to be "metamorphosed."

And how does it occur? Paul says, "Do this by the renewing of your mind." For there to be victorious transformation rather than defeating conformity, there must be renewing thoughts. The primary battleground is the mind—that inner part of our being where we decide who we are and where we stand. Only a radically different mindset can equip folks like us to stand alone when we're outnumbered.

day Two

# Standing Tall When Tested

"And they were for testing Israel, to find out if they would obey the commandments of the Lord, which He had commanded their fathers through Moses" (Judges 3:4).

Let's go back to the Book of Judges and take a look at the situation when the Hebrews encountered the Canaanites. God had warned the Hebrews that the Canaanites would be all around them, and He had told them the reason they would be there. Read Judges 3:4. The Canaanites were there for one reason—to be a test!

Three things characterized the Hebrews' lives when they moved into the land.

1. *They were alone and uncertain.* They got into the land, but then they began to wonder, *Joshua's dead. Moses is dead. Wonder where we go from here?* They felt insecure and uncertain. The world *feeds* on uncertainty and aloneness.

"And all that generation also were gathered to their fathers; and there arose another generation after them who did not know the Lord, nor yet the work which He had done for Israel" (Judges 2:10).

2. *Those Hebrews were inexperienced and vulnerable.* They had not seen firsthand God's mighty works in Egypt and the wilderness. The generation Moses and Joshua had addressed had died off (Judg. 2:10). Two things were true of those new folks: they didn't know the Lord, and they didn't know what He had done in the previous years. They lacked the knowledge of what brought them there; they had no awareness of what their liberty had really cost!

3. *They were surrounded and outnumbered.*

**Check one box for each question below and on page 159.**

Compare your experiences with the Hebrews'. Has God tested you in similar ways?

❑ rarely          ❑ sometimes          ❑ often

Have you been placed in circumstances where you felt uncertain and alone?

❑ rarely ❑ sometimes ❑ often

Have you found yourself living off the miraculous spiritual experiences of others?

❑ rarely ❑ sometimes ❑ often

Do you feel surrounded and outnumbered by worldly people and influences?

❑ rarely ❑ sometimes ❑ often

**If God is testing you, read carefully Dr. Swindoll's "Three Encouragements for Standing Tall" at the end of Day 2.**

Now read Judges 3:3,5.

How do the Israelites react? Again, there are three reactions.

*First of all, there was lack of total obedience.* In Deuteronomy 7:1-2, we read where the Lord had in essence said, "Don't let any of them live. Annihilate them." But look what happened. Read Judges 1:19,21,27-32. Again and again, right down the line we find that God's people failed to destroy the inhabitants of the land. Finally we come to verse 33 where we read that the tribe of Naphtali "lived among the Canaanites." Did you catch that? The enemy is no longer down in the valley. Hebrews and Canaanites are now *living* together. What exactly happened? *They lacked total obedience.* They rationalized around it; they mentally imagined obedience, but they acted out compromise.

*Second, they suffered a loss of spiritual distinctiveness.* Because they lacked total obedience, they decided to leave the Canaanites in the valley. Instead of destroying them, the Hebrews used the Canaanites as forced labor, but eventually the Israelites themselves bowed down to the Canaanite gods. Read Judges 2:10-12. Through compromise their spiritual distinctiveness was eroded.

*The third Israelite reaction was a looseness of marital ties.* Read Judges 3:6. Never fails, does it? Let a nation drift morally and before long the same values or lack of values will move right into the home. The Israelites chose immoral friends, and before long their marital ties were loosened.

"These nations are: the five lords of the Philistines and all the Canaanites and the Sidonians and the Hivites who lived in Mount Lebanon, from Mount Baal-hermon as far as Lebo-hamath. . . . And the sons of Israel lived among the Canaanites, the Hittites, the Amorites, the Perizzites, the Hivites, and the Jebusites" (Judges 3:3,5).

"Then the sons of Israel did evil in the sight of the Lord, and served the Baals, and they forsook the Lord, the God of their fathers, who had brought them out of the land of Egypt, and followed other gods from among the gods of the peoples who were around them, and bowed themselves down to them; thus they provoked the Lord to anger" (Judges 2:10-12).

"And they took their daughters for themselves as wives, and gave their own daughters to their sons, and served their gods" (Judges 3:6).

**Complete the scale below to compare your reactions with those of the Israelites. 1 = not true of me. 5 = very true of me.**

1 2 3 4 5    I imagine obedience but find myself rationalizing disobedience.

1 2 3 4 5    I have eroded my spiritual distinctiveness through compromise.

1 2 3 4 5    I have drifted morally so that I've weakened my relationships.

**If you scored 10 or more points, what will you do to follow Paul's advice to renew your mind, where the primary battle begins. Reread Romans 12:2.**

---

### THREE ENCOURAGEMENTS FOR STANDING TALL

Allow me to offer three suggestions for standing tall.

First: *Standing tall starts with the way we think.* It has to do with the *mind.* As I've said so often, being a person of inner strength is really a mental factor: excellence starts in the mind. It has to do with the way we think about God, ourselves, and others. Then it grows into the way we think about business, the way we think about dating, the way we think about marriage and the family, the way we think about the system that is designed to destroy faith and bring us down to a lower standard.

Second: *Standing tall calls for strong discipline.* This has to do with the *will.* Disciplining the eyes, the ears, the hands, the feet. Keeping moral tabs on ourselves, refusing to let down the standards. People of strength know how to turn right thinking into action—even when insistent feelings don't agree.

Third: *Standing tall limits your choice of personal friends.* This has to do with *relationships.* What appears harmless can prove to be dangerous. Perhaps this is as important as the other two factors combined. Cultivate wrong friendships and you're a goner. This is why we are warned not to be deceived regarding the danger of wrong associations. Without realizing it, we could be playing with fire.

"For whatever was written in earlier times was written for our instruction, that through perseverance and the encouragement of the Scriptures we might have hope" (Romans 15:4).

# Standing Firm When Discouraged

Discouragement is just plain *awful*.

When we get discouraged, we temporarily lose our perspective. Little things become mammoth. A slight irritation seems huge. Motivation is drained away and, worst of all, hope departs.

There is a magnificent thought nestled in Romans 15:4. To the surprise of some folks, the promise is connected to a major reason God has preserved the Old Testament. God had an ultimate goal in mind: that "we might have hope." And what is it that leads to such a goal? Two things: "perseverance" and "encouragement" from the Scriptures. Through endurance and through encouragement from the Scriptures we can gain hope.

What a priceless nugget of truth. What I find here is the scriptural basis for encouragement. God offers instruction, but then it's our move. We must *accept* His instruction and *apply* it to our lives. Then, and only then, can we expect to cash in on the benefits of His instruction. So you see, application is the essential link between instruction and change.

## GUIDELINES FOR HANDLING DISCOURAGEMENT

Let's return to the Old Testament Book of Judges for a brief look at the life of a man you may have never even heard of. He was an ancient eagle type named Gideon. Read Judges 6:2-5.

How demoralizing! Not only were the Israelites stripped of their *homes* (v. 2), but they had *no peace* either (vv. 3-4). When they planted crops to grow food for their families, the Midianites, along with the Amalekites, invaded. They mercilessly destroyed the crops after taking just enough produce for themselves. So the Israelites began to starve. On top of all their other troubles, now they had *no sustenance* (v. 5).

That's enough about the problem. What we really need are specific suggestions that get us back on track. I find no less than five such guidelines woven through the biblical narrative concerning the Israelites and the Midianites.

"And the power of Midian prevailed against Israel. Because of Midian the sons of Israel made for themselves the dens which were in the mountains and the caves and the strongholds. For it was when Israel had sown, that the Midianites would come up with the Amalekites and the sons of the east and go against them. So they would camp against them and destroy the produce of the earth as far as Gaza, and leave no sustenance in Israel as well as no sheep, ox, or donkey. For they would come up with their livestock and their tents, they would come in like locusts for number, both they and their camels were innumerable; and they came into the land to devastate it" (Judges 6:2-5).

**161**

1. *Openly acknowledge what caused your condition.* Read Judges 6:6-10. Hold nothing back! Even though it may be painful, total honesty is important. Openly admit that you have failed to stand alone as a true child of God and therefore you have begun to live like a heathen Midianite.

Are you ready for some super-encouraging news? When we openly acknowledge our condition before our God, He won't reject us. Nor will He put us on probation and watch us squirm. On the contrary, we'll find the Lord to be explicitly interested and compassionate, quick to forgive.

2. *Focus directly on the Lord, not on the odds against you.* Read Judges 6:12-16. Everything depends on where your focus is. You must discipline yourself to focus directly on the Lord, not on the odds!

At first all Gideon could see were odds. Finally, he heard the Lord's word, "Have I not sent you?" Then Gideon says, "I'm the youngest." He felt incapable. He felt as if he were not the man to do the job. And the Lord said, "Look, I'll be with you. Even though you're one man, you'll do it." And He promised him, "Peace to you, do not fear; you shall not die." How comforting!

> "You will not stand alone when out-numbered or stand tall when tested or stand firm when discouraged if your focus remains on the odds."
> –Charles Swindoll

Get this straight and never forget it: You will not stand alone when outnumbered or stand tall when tested or stand firm when discouraged if your focus remains on the odds. Your eyes must be trained on the Lord.

3. *Declare your allegiance publicly.* Read Judges 6:33-35. Somehow that trumpet blast announced something significant to the people in those days. When Gideon declared his allegiance publicly, God honored his courage. And others fell in rank behind him.

Have you made it known to others where you stand spiritually? I'm not suggesting a trumpet, but I am suggesting a clarion communication of your allegiance to Christ as Lord.

4. *Remember that God prefers to work through a remnant.* Read Judges 7:2-7. God does His best work, it seems, when those who serve Him are fewer than those against Him. As a result of the strange strategy, God used Gideon to turn the tide. He won the battle. He led God's people to victory.

5. *Do not accept the glory after God uses your life.* Read Judges 8:22-23. The Israelites were grateful. In fact, they invited Gideon to be their leader. Our most vulnerable moment, as you may have heard before, is immediately after a great victory. With masterful restraint, Gideon models godly (and rare) humility.

Today God is still looking for Gideons. But there is one major problem: They are scarce. You may be that one person God wants to use in your sphere of influence. And if it is discouragement that is keeping you from being totally available to Him, come to terms with whatever brought it on. Get rid of it so that God can launch you and use you greatly.

### How do you typically deal with disappointment or discouragement? Underline.

- try to learn something from the experience
- blame the other person
- shut down like a clam
- take it out on an innocent person (or animal)
- brood; sulk; get angry
- pray for the other person(s) involved

### What will you change based on Dr. Swindoll's guidelines? _____

# Standing Strong When Tempted

When Samson makes his first appearance on the scriptural scene, we immediately detect a character flaw. He possesses a lustful, passionate drive that he does not attempt to restrain—neither now nor later. Read Judges 14:1-3,7. I think it is highly significant that the first four recorded words from Samson's lips are, "I saw a woman." That is the story of his life. *He focused on the wrong objective.* Samson's focusing on the wrong objectives proved to be his downfall. First, he focused on physical appearance and little else. Second, he focused on pleasing himself and no one else. Twice we read in the biblical account that the Philistine woman "looked good" to the young Israelite.

Now there is a second characteristic of Samson that was also unfavorable. *He handled his leisure carelessly.* Do you remember what the angel said about the purpose of his life? He was to "begin to deliver Israel." Seems to me he is getting sidetracked. So far he has spent very little time delivering Israel. The man is mainly into pleasing himself. Read Judges 14:10-14. Hold it! Here's a guy who should have been soaring, beginning to deliver Israel, as God had commanded. But what is he doing? Posing riddles to these ding-a-lings from Philistia! To Samson, leisure was synonymous with lust.

It was bad enough that Samson fanned the flame of lust, but in addition to that, he continued to run with a bad bunch. This combination inevitably spells disaster. Now we come to Samson's third unfavorable characteristic: *He developed a close alliance with the wrong crowd.* Complete corruption was just around the corner, thanks to the bad company Samson kept. All that time spent with the Philistines was the catalyst—the major force—that caused him to fall prey to Delilah's advances (16:4-14).

Samson's fourth major flaw: *He didn't take his vow seriously.* Finally, Samson poured it all out; he told her *everything:* "A razor has never come on my head. . . . If I am shaved, then my strength will leave me and I shall become weak and be like any other man" (v. 17). What was the secret of Samson's defeat? Simply this: He didn't choose to say NO to temptation.

Heroes, listen up! Spiritual leaders, pay attention! My fellow eagle, take heed! "[Every man] is tempted when he is carried away and enticed by his own lust" (James 1:14). The Greek word translated "enticed" means "to lure by a bait." The bait is dropped, and the fish, seeing the bait, is lured away from its safe hiding place. Likewise, we move closer to grab the bait of pleasure, and as we do so God becomes quite unreal. In fact, He's momentarily *forgotten.* The bait is real; God is not. And for that brief moment we are thinking of one thing—how pleasurable it will be to grab that morsel.

Let me mention another very practical thing about temptation. I have found that if I can stop the process fairly early, I'm safe. But if I leave my hiding place and venture toward the bait, there is a point of no return. I cannot turn around. If I go that far, I'm sunk.

That's the way it is with us, and that's the way it was with Samson. He pandered with leisure and played with the wrong crowd and messed around with the bait so much he could not turn around. At that point God had become totally unreal to him. With God blocked out, "He told her all that was in his heart." No wonder we read that he didn't even know the Spirit of God had departed from him.

**Write *agree* or *disagree* for the following statements.**

_____ Temptation is not regarded as a serious problem by our society.

_____ An adult audience means that any adult, Christian or not, should be able to see any movie or TV show.

_____ An innocent flirtation at work doesn't have to lead anywhere.

_____ When we are focused on the wrong crowd and/or dubious activities, God is momentarily forgotten.

## THE INEVITABLE CONSEQUENCES

Two inevitable consequences follow in the wake of those who play the fool and yield to temptation's alluring bait. Both expose lies from the world system.

First: *We are weakened, not strengthened.* The world says that a playboy lifestyle will make you strong. Ever heard words like this? "By being exposed to temptations, by getting up close to lust, you learn you can handle those temptations." No, Samson shows us that such a lifestyle really weakens us. If we don't break away, it isn't long before the weakness becomes an addiction, leading to a tragic end.

Second: *We become enslaved, not freed.* The system says, "Free love frees you up." Well, that's a lie. It actually puts you into bondage. Samson became a victim of the very ones he was supposed to conquer.

## AN EAGLELIKE STRATEGY FOR FLIGHT

Here is a straightforward, succinct strategy for a soaring flight.

First: *Our natural focus must be counteracted.* Openly confess your weakness. Hide nothing.

Second: *Our leisure time must be guarded.* Cultivate a plan, perhaps an exercise program, an intensive reading program, a hobby, a series of practical projects that occupy your time. Watch out for those video movies piped into your room! If necessary, keep the television off. And stay away from the magazine rack.

Third: *Our close companions must be screened.* Take a good look at your circle of friends. Do an honest evaluation of those with whom you spend personal time. I can offer you a principle you can bank on:

> "Until you clean up your companionships, you'll never clean up your life."
> —Charles Swindoll

**165**

Until you clean up your companionships, you'll never clean up your life. You may want to. You may have sincere desires and the highest of ambitions, but if you plan to soar, pick your partners with great care. Remember, eagles fly with only a few other eagles—never in flocks.

Fourth: *Our vow to God must be upheld.* Just as jealously as we would guard the marriage vows, we're to guard our promises to God and our commitment to purity. Remember Romans 12:1-2 is your primary vow.

## day Five

# Who's Appraising Your Excellence?

> "A commitment to excellence in the Christian life is neither popular nor easy. But it is essential."
> –Charles Swindoll

Mediocrity is fast becoming the by-word of our times. Status quo averages are held up as all we can now expect. It is my firm conviction that those who impact and reshape the world are the ones committed to living above the level of mediocrity. A commitment to excellence in the Christian life is neither popular nor easy. But it is essential. A commitment to excellence touches the externals of appearance, communication, and products just as much as the internals of attitude, vision, taste, humor, compassion, determination, and zest for life.

**How has your commitment to excellence affected the externals of your life?** _____

**How has it affected the internal parts of you?**

_____

The Bible states, "if there be any excellence . . . set your mind on these things" (Phil. 4:8). In the final analysis, it is the living Lord who appraises our excellence, it is He whom we must please and serve, honor, and adore. For His eyes only we commit ourselves to living above the level of mediocrity. He deserves our very best; nothing more, nothing less, nothing else. That alone is excellence.

**Have you made the commitment to Christian excellence—nothing less, nothing else? Write a prayer in the margin stating your feelings. Be honest with God. He knows the truth!**

# leader Guide

## Before the Session

1. Prepare a short lecture on Elijah's experiences in 1 Kings 19: 1-13.
2. Optional: Enlist someone to play the role of Samson telling his story from the material in Day 4. Set the time limit in advance.

## During the Session

1. Welcome participants and thank them for their participation in this first quarter of *MasterWork*. Announce next quarter's study. Open with prayer requests and prayer.
2. Review last week's lesson. Ask, *What were the two habits that we sought to break?* (apathetic indifference and joyless selfishness) Provide an overview of this week's lesson. Ask someone to name the four areas in which we must stand courageously if we are going to defeat mediocrity. (outnumbered, tested, discouraged, tempted)
3. Discuss each of Dr. Swindoll's six observations from Romans 12: 1-2 under Day 1. Begin by reading the passage. Ask, *Why is it almost impossible to stand alone morally and spiritually when you are outnumbered*?
4. Deliver your short lecture from 1 Kings. Select a volunteer to read 1 Kings 19:14-18 and summarize why Elijah felt outnumbered. Ask: *What was his mood? What was God's reaction? Should Christians ever feel outnumbered?*
5. Ask: *Without giving names, do you know a new believer who stood strong against the world but sputtered to a stop in a matter of months? What do you think happened?* Read Dr. Swindoll's statements in his first observation in Day 1.
6. From his second observation, ask, *What is the difference in being a non-conformist and not conforming to worldly standards?*
7. On a writing surface, draw a vertical line making two columns. Label the left column *conform* and the right column *transform*. Ask the group to name as many synonyms as possible under each heading. Ask, *If these words are very different, why do polls fail to pick up many lifestyle differences between Christians and non-Christians?*

Do your class members feel they are waging a losing war against worldly influences? If so, today's study is a reminder that one person plus God is a majority. Challenge members to stand courageously.

NOTES

8. According to the material Dr. Swindoll gave in Day 2, ask volunteers to list ways the Hebrews were being tested. Ask, *Do you think Christians today are tested in similar ways?* Then ask, *What are some of the many rewards of standing tall? What are the sacrifices of standing tall?*

9. Have members recall the title of Day 3. Point out that one of the purposes for the local church is to surround Christians with friends and co-laborers so we will encourage each other and not lose heart. Ask someone to read 1 Samuel 14: 6-16. Point out verse 7 as an example of encouragement.

10. Ask, *Does the story of Jonathan and the armor-bearer reflect the six guidelines Dr. Swindoll gives for handling discouragement?*

11. Optional: Introduce the character of Samson and let him tell his story. Or, ask the class to turn to Judges 14. Read the passage using Dr. Swindoll's exposition from Day 4. Emphasize the five points in italics.

12. Ask someone to name the two consequences of yielding to temptation listed under Day 4. (We are weakened and enslaved.) As time permits, form four groups to discuss one each of the four eaglelike strategies for flight at the end of Day 4. Call for group reports after 3 minutes.

13. Close today's session by asking the question that is the title of Day 5. Emphasize that if we are to become Christlike, by definition we are choosing to live above the level of mediocrity.

14. Pray sentence prayers around the circle and close the prayer time.

15. Distribute to learners copies of the new *MasterWork* books for next quarter's studies.

## After the Session

1. Read next week's content and complete the learning activities. Follow the suggestions in "Before the Session."

2. Pray for each member of your class by name. Pray especially for anyone who may be feeling discouragement. Others may be wrestling with the issue of conforming to worldly standards. Make yourself available after class for personal ministry.

3. Contact visitors and members who may have missed class recently. Let them know that a new study is beginning next week.